Song of Sight

An Introduction to Soul Passage Midwifery

Patricia L'Dara
Soul Passage Midwife

ISBN: 978-0-692-84181-5

Copyright © 2017 by Patricia L'Dara
First e-book version © 2012

All rights reserved including the right to reproduce this book or portions thereof in any form whatsoever.

Printed by Lulu Press

You can reach the author, Patricia L'Dara, at:
www.soulpassagemidwife.com.

Cover Artwork and Design: Valerie Chelonis

Story Behind the Painting: Isis-Mari, Womb of Heaven. "Enter the Temple of Isis-Mari and experience sacred space, a gift from the Goddess, where the Divine Feminine is honored. Realize your inner divinity and wholeness. Come, enter the Temple of Your Heart." Within the Temple sits the Goddess Isis-Mari, who is Sky Goddess and Earth Mother, the Divine Feminine Creatrix energy that nourishes and sustains us all. She lives in your heart. Come home to her loving embrace.

Valerie Chelonis is an artist, visionary, and healer. She has been involved in metaphysics and alternative healing for over 30 years. Valerie has been gifted with the ability to bring forth different forms of light, love and energy into her creative life, primarily in the forms of painting and jewelry. She can be reached at eaglewoman87508@yahoo.com.

*for the Sacred
Feminine*

in memory of my mother Jane

in honor of my daughter Serena

ACKNOWLEDGEMENTS

To the many beautiful Spirit Beings who guide, inspire, and make this work possible.

Parmahansa Yogananda
Archangel Azreal
Archangel Gabrielle
Butterfly Maiden
Sush Al'Mundra
Archangel Jophiel
Archangel Sandalphon
Dana
Metatron
White Eagle
Archangel Michael
Quan Yin
Kali
Spirit of Gaia
Nature Spirits

To the amazing souls, who have trusted deeply and shared their passages with me. It is a most profound honor to engage your concerns, insights, messages, and journeys.

To Lama Kalsang and Chief Cloudpiler for encouragement on the path of this work.

To Sharry Edwards, Dr. Steve Koral and Dr. Ken Gerdes, earth angels who saved my life this time around.

To friends who read my early efforts and gave important feedback: Suzanne Plave, Yvonne Short, Paula Henderson, Linda Borakove, and Brad Hartman.

To Maia Nartoomid, Arlen Bock, and Simeon Nartoomid, who felt it was time to write this book when I wasn't even thinking about it.

To Maria Dancing Heart Hoaglund, who brought the world incredible insights about preparing for a death transition.

To my wonderful editor, Jennifer Phelps, whose insights and questions clarified many a paragraph! What a joyous journey we had together.

TABLE OF CONTENTS

PROLOGUE	9
Quote 1	11
Quote 2	13
Quote 3	15
PART I: ACROSS THE VEIL	17
Introduction	19
Chapter 1: Sight Awakening	23
Chapter 2: Sacred Transformation	37
Chapter 3: Souls Who Have Crossed the Threshold	97
PART II: OPENING TO SOUL PASSAGE MIDWIFERY	111
Introduction	113
Chapter 4: Releasing, Deepening, Expanding	119
Chapter 5: Holding the Presence	145
Chapter 6: Meditative Focus	161
Chapter 7: Death Passage as Creative Process	173
Chapter 8: Interdimensional Communication	195
PART III: PERSONAL APPLICATION	219
Chapter 9: Living Tapestry of Light	223
Concluding Remarks	249
EPILOGUE	253
Bibliography	257
About the Author	261

Prologue

A death passage is a sacred birth celebrated by Spirit. While we may grieve the loss of a loved one, we can also celebrate the higher vibratory emergence of the soul, which one's death passage signifies.

A Soul Passage Midwife is one who assists in creating a graceful transition in the spirit world for a soul returning to the Higher Realms.

Soul Passage Midwifery has its roots in ancient times. Priestesses were trained in the arts and mystical skills necessary for assisting souls to pass GENTLY through portal ways. In current times, not only have the ancient spiritual arts of mystery schools disappeared, but also people have lost conscious awareness of their souls and their lessons. With the revival of these ancient arts, people will again feel keen connection with their souls, understand the process of death passage and feel connected with Source. It will be much to the advantage of all to have this understanding.

Part I:

Across the Veil

Part I:
Introduction

Eternal life is a large concept inviting deep understanding. What exactly might these words mean in the context of losing someone to a death passage? If we could each paint a more accurate picture of the Great Beyond, might we find incredible solace in this better understanding? While millions of Americans profess to believe in eternal life, when a loved one dies, often there is only the aspect of loss that confronts the psyche. Grief explodes like a tenacious octopus strangling our senses and our hearts. We are then left to grapple with this assault by ourselves devoid of the deep spiritual insight that is our birthright. Somewhere in our collective psyche, eternal life seems to have gotten packed away in a box and put in the attic, as if it is not relevant to our purpose or to our people. Nothing could be further from the truth. It is relevant now and in our future.

If we wish to internalize the concept of eternal life, we have to have a belief that feels tangible to explore that gives relevance to the Unseen World. In modern times, we use these words as an intellectual concept only, which fits nicely with an image of a highly educated society, but does nothing to support our loved ones and families at the time of a most challenging passage. The raw truth is that each one of us goes through this passage. Rather than an afterthought, it is of the highest priority to garner as accurate an understanding as possible and integrate it into our personal and collective belief systems. We do not have to wait until it is "our time" to give closer inspection. In fact, the sooner we give this belief our full personal attention, the better it is for each of us as individuals and for our families.

Our souls are connected with the earth and with eternal life. This core essence or eternal aspect of our nature finds the return Home a joyful experience. Thus, connecting with this aspect for each of us provides a key to releasing fear and embracing the new life. The challenge is that there isn't the awareness that this is a viable path. This path can be taken by anyone because each of us is an aspect of the All with a foot already in eternity.

In the pages that follow are messages from souls who have crossed over, accounts of my participation in the process of crossing over as a daughter and Soul Passage Midwife, as well as perspectives to help us examine the topic of death passage through different eyes. The doors that can open with this study lead to a much greater understanding about who we are and where we are going. This weaving of seen and Unseen Worlds at the time of death passage brings a deeper understanding of eternal life, as well as an incredible beauty that does not fade.

My vision of the world is a perspective in which when death draws near, we can come to recognize that the dying person has accomplished what he or she has come to do and is now getting ready to graduate from his or her experience on earth. We might even substitute the word "graduation" for "death."

Maria Dancing Heart Hoaglund (*The Most Important Day of Your Life: Are You Ready?*)

Chapter One
Sight Awakening

My Mother

October 1993

Bethesda, Maryland

Agonizing despair grips my every cell. "Why do I know nothing about this?" is the phrase that churns over and over in my mind. My mom is dying. She is in excruciating pain. Also, she is terrified. Engulfed by massive waves of tears, I am immobilized. I do not know what to do or how to help. I have never before been with someone who is dying. Feeling utterly defeated, I offer a simple prayer, "Please help her."

Just four days ago, our eyes were locked into a loving gaze hour after hour. Profound joy swept through our pores. Delicate golden light visibly streamed through Mom's window. Sacred peace was so apparent in her hospital room that everyone who entered abruptly stopped. Where did that all go?

A week ago the doctor said, "Your mother is in remission." What happened to that pronouncement? Or what about the experience three days ago when Mom was whole, perfect and well with her brilliant blue eyes dancing ecstatically? What robbed her of that?

Despair. Profound joy. Defeat. Sacred peace. My mind ricochets trying to make sense of all of this. It gets nowhere. Finally, the sobbing subsides. Desperate to create some measure of comfort for my mom, I return to her room.

Expecting the worst when I step through the door, I am once again shocked by what greets my eyes. The orchids pulse majestically with their royal purple and snowy-white colors. Their living subtle essence radiates all the way across the ceiling and over to Mom's bed, like exotic crystals reflecting the bright sunlight. Angels filled with vast love surround her. The exquisite beauty emanating from my mother is astounding. Just moments ago all I could see was a ravaged woman struggling for breath. Now, she is brimming with youth and vitality. The brilliance is palpable. "How can this be?" I wonder. Yet, there is no time to contemplate.

I quickly move to my mother's bedside and begin spontaneously singing. It is a force that compels me, not my mind thinking I should do this. The severe pain makes it unbearable for her to be touched. Singing becomes the container that holds us, bringing life and closeness in the moment. For two straight hours I sing of the joy we have shared, thank her for all she has done, and let her know that she will go first and then help each of us when it is our time. I also sing hymns and songs that she loved. A dear friend joins our song and we become a loving triad.

As Mom's time draws near, I feel the intensity of the energy change dramatically. The song moves more and more quickly, with a gospel-like rhythm. Then, suddenly, I find myself immersed in another realm, a realm that could be called by many names, such as the Greater World, the Expanded World, the Subtle Realms, the Other Side, or the Great Beyond. I don't know how I got here, but I am walking in an extremely thick, dense fog with my mother in my arms. At first I have no idea where we are going, but then, oddly, it feels like I have been here before. In fact, I finally realize, this feels more familiar than normal earth living. In this realm, things move quickly and are improvisational in nature, requiring full concentration.

At the bedside, I continue singing to my mom. I am fully aware that I am both at the bedside and in the Greater World. My essence has expanded to accommodate this need. Our souls walk steadfastly through the Greater World. As we continue in the dense fog, we surprisingly come to a large, golden bridge. Without hesitation, we begin walking over the bridge. My mother and I do not talk. We are immersed in the Sacred Silence that rings with purity and living intelligence.

From the profound depths of the Silence, splendid angelic music begins to surround, infuse and embrace us. We become one with each note. Our steps become very deliberate and slow. About midway across the bridge, the fog suddenly clears and the Christ appears in a long, hooded white robe. He is radiating a gentle, peaceful, joyous welcome. No words can describe the vastness of Love that pours into us at this moment. As I pass my mother to the outstretched arms of the Christ, I am filled with Celestial Celebration. Tears of gratitude roll down my cheeks. My mother is Home. I am amazed and grateful. Also, I know in the deepest part of my being that my mother is fine. Her soul lives on. What a comfort.

Abruptly, my older brother comes to the bedside to ask if I would like to get something to eat. I shake my head no. My mother's body is still breathing. Shortly after the family leaves, I feel my throat choked with dryness. Since I know that my mother's soul is safely on the Other Side, I decide to quickly get a drink of water. When I am in the hallway returning to Mom's room, I hear my name over the loudspeaker. I race back to her room. Her body has stopped breathing.

The day following, I am in my parents' bedroom gathering things to take to the funeral home. Exhaustion keeps encouraging me to lie down. I am fighting it because I feel I do not have time to rest. Finally, I succumb. As my eyes start to close, my mother appears! Our eyes meet with tears of overwhelming joy. Just yesterday I was sobbing in agonizing despair because I did not know what to expect, what to do or how to help. Today, my mother and I happily communicate telepathically across worlds. She is most grateful for the beautiful assistance during her crossing and has returned to say thank you. When we part, it is with the knowledge that Eternal Life gently holds us always. We will visit again.

My Father

October 1994

Nederland, Colorado

The exquisite fall Colorado weather finds us preparing for my dad's transition. Just one year ago, my mother crossed. Remembering the anxiety prior to her soul passage, I feel grateful that I understand the process. Armed with the experience I had with my mother, preparations are simple and conscious. Since Dad is at home and we are together, his spiritual insights along the way help to inform the process. There is a gentle acceptance of his changes.

For weeks our home has been a veritable cathedral filled with angels, masters and ancestors. This convergence renders the birth of each day as swelling celebration. In such company and surrounded by incredible beauty in each moment, I cannot be sad. Of course, if my dad were well and could stay, I would want him to do just that. But, his body is failing day by day; something that he finds frustrating and disturbing.

Two months ago, my mother appeared to me to say, "Your father will go soon and he will go quickly." Thus, I have been preparing since September. Not long ago, my dad and I talked. He told me that he did not want to cause me the pain that he experienced with my mother's sudden death. I gently let him know how much I appreciated his deep love for me. Then I explained to him that if his left side became paralyzed, as was his right side, I would no longer be able to care for him. Moving him to a nursing facility would be far more painful for me than helping him to transition from our home. When he fully realized that he could join my mother in the Higher Realms from within the safety and comfort of our home, grateful tears formed in his eyes.

Many people help to make caring for my dad possible. Hospice comes daily up into the mountains where everyone said they would never go. We have a nurse, a music therapist, a spiritual attendant, a certified nursing assistant, and a much loved volunteer. My husband works just twenty minutes away. Also, there is someone who sits with Dad each night because I need to rest a bit. This little community brings loving faces to sing, pray, bathe, grocery shop, and monitor Dad's situation. Dad greets each visitor with great enthusiasm when the appointed hour arrives. There is a sweet rhythm to our days as people come and go. Spiritual healer Arlen Bock helps Dad with any challenges along the way. We all grow very close during the course of our months together.

As diligently as people on this side of the veil are working to help my father, spirit beings on the other side of the veil are vigilant in helping him to prepare. His vibration needs to be attuned to the correct frequency so this transition can be smooth and gentle. My father is very receptive and requires dedicated silence in his room so he can focus.

At 2:00 a.m. Dad clamors for me to come to his room, something he has done only once before. I come downstairs immediately to see what he needs. Dad says, "I can't live with you anymore." I ask where he is going, to which he replies, "I am going to live with God." We smile a knowing smile at each other. I then give him a kiss on his forehead as he promptly falls asleep.

Throughout these days and nights, I sometimes catch glimpses of the spirit beings in the house. Recently, I felt delighted to see my paternal grandmother who passed when I was in my early twenties. I know that my mother often sits in the chair in Dad's room, intently focused on his process. Today, while I am downstairs putting laundry in the washer, Swami Yogananda, Swami Sri Yukesteswar and the Christ appear before me with the message, "The time is at hand." Dropping the laundry, I bound upstairs to my father. He is not quite ready this minute, but I know it is very soon. Today is October 28.

The morning of October 31, Dad is peacefully resting when I suddenly hear him call to me. All of the spirit beings are with him, along with my mother and his mother, so he does not need me to escort him. Within minutes of my entry into his room, he bids farewell. We hold a candlelight vigil in our home through the night that brings comfort and extraordinary inspiration.

The following day I sit in Dad's room and wonder how long I might let his body rest. It is unusually warm this year, more like summer than fall, so I am concerned about decay. I ask my parents if they could somehow let me know. Just as I am about to go to the kitchen to get a drink of water, both of my parents appear to me beaming! Joyful smiles are shared and we all breathe in deeply the nectar of soul awareness. I also gently cry tears of relief. They let me know that they are both fine, they thank me and they assure me that the body can go whenever it works for me.

Gleaning Understanding

What is one to make of these encounters? My parents were not people who would have believed in these types of experiences. Like many in our Western society, they believed that mere humans could never attain such levels. Yet somehow, even though I had never had a firsthand experience with dying before my parents died, I was then and am now apparently fluent with its processes. How is that possible? I believe it is because my soul carries the imprint of this work. A soul's work goes on regardless of the current popular beliefs of the culture. We have much to learn from our souls and must listen intently if we are to change our perceptions of dying.

My mother's passing was a life altering experience for me. At the deepest level I realized that there is absolutely nothing in a soul passage to cause alarm. No one need ever be terrified as was my mother. No one need ever experience the severe agony that I faced. Lack of information about the actual crossing was at the core of the agony and terror for my mother and me. Others can benefit from our experience.

My father's passing was an incredibly peaceful process including the time leading up to the moment and following his transition. This was possible because of the understandings I gained with my mother. It takes only one experience with conscious dying to help one comprehend that there are ways to practice that are helpful, which change the experience for everyone.

A bridge to the Other Side that is created with conscious awareness brings comfort step by step. The person crossing, families and professionals can learn how to see through different eyes to embrace this deeply sacred transition and true Cosmic Celebration.

Insights for Those Preparing to Cross Over:
- Spirit diligently prepares and uniquely welcomes each individual soul.
- There is nothing to fear.
- The dying process is preparation for changing vibration and remembering our souls.
- Souls are situated on the Other Side before the body quits breathing.
- Telepathic communication is natural and normal on the Other Side.
- Souls are fluent in the ways of the next world; one does not have to worry.
- It is possible for loved ones to accompany a soul across the threshold.

- It is possible to communicate with loved ones on earth after one arrives on the Other Side.

Insights for Families and Professionals:
- Personal experience with the process of dying brings skill and understanding.
- Singing to loved ones helps them and helps families to connect with their own souls.
- Prayer and song accompany loved ones across the threshold.
- Accompanying someone across the threshold is improvisational in nature.
- Soul awareness helps tremendously to mitigate grief.
- Those preparing for dying will let us know if they prefer singing, verbal prayer or silence by their receptivity.
- Change in vibration is a natural and normal process.
- A soul passage is a Cosmic Celebration of the highest order.
- Remembering that the soul or core essence is eternal in nature is an essential understanding.

Conclusion

As a result of the experiences with crossing the threshold with my parents, I believe that it is critically important for our culture to engage in conversation about the process of dying. My parents' generation did not talk about many things and certainly did not discuss the topic of death. It feels as if their belief was almost superstitious in nature. Perhaps people then had concern that mentioning death would hasten its appearance into their lives. This misperception can change. Through talking and sharing such experiences, we can create a much deeper understanding of something, through which we each must pass.

People the world around have amazing spiritual experiences at the time of death. Often, however, these experiences are dismissed as imagination or wishful thinking. My mind suggested the idea of wishful thinking the day following the profound experience with my mother. This aspect of mind is very tenacious so one has to be vigilant in casting out such thoughts. In accepting the higher truth, I was able to see and hear my mom say, "Thank you for your deeply loving assistance." Also, through embracing the reality of the Eternal World, I am able to continue to have connection with my mother's soul. Once one has such a peaceful and vibrant encounter with death, any fear whatever dissipates.

Experiencing my mother's death opened the door to conscious dying. Thus, my father's preparation and exit were quiet and gentle. No agony. No terror. Although at first Dad was unwilling to talk about his death, as he moved closer to crossing the threshold, he was able to honestly share his beautiful spiritual experiences. I was able to celebrate his mini-steps towards his soul life. Radiant Beauty enters readily through such moments. I feel that this knowing brings profound peace within for the person crossing and for the family.

Spirit stands ever ready to assist people in remembering soul awareness and the Expanded Realms (or Subtle Realms or Unseen World) at the time of a transition. As the knowledge of death as celebration, death as birth, and death as sacred transformation is passed from one person to the next; it helps enliven the ever-present Song of Sight.

With the dissolution of the walls of forgetting within you, you will remember who you truly are. You become integrated with your greater self and feel the lightness and vastness of it. Thus death, contrary to popular opinion, is a very wonderful experience.

Barbara Brennan (*Hands of Light*)

Chapter Two
Sacred Transformation

Following the experience with my mother, I discovered that I could be present in Expanded Consciousness with anyone crossing the veil either in person or long distance, which means I can connect with the soul in the same room or across the world. In ancient Greece, someone who had this ability was called a Psychopomp or End-of-Life Doula. Such a person, or soul, ensures a graceful transition and bears the responsibility of safe escort for the soul to reach the highest vibration within that soul's awareness. This can also include assistance for souls entering as infants into the world. As a sacred endeavor, accompanying departing or arriving souls is beyond any specific religion, yet it can be inclusive of all religions. The term Soul Passage Midwife is what I am calling this type of work today.

I most frequently work long distance with souls simply because of the last minute nature of the experience. It is not unusual for me to accompany a soul for a specific portion of the journey either before or after the actual crossing. In this way, messages can be transmitted to loved ones and/or for humanity-at-large. The singular requirement is the desire of the soul making the journey. If a being would like accompaniment, then s/he will invite my presence for whatever portion of the passage s/he would like. If not, no matter the desires of the family, there will be no contact. The following message from Mary G. exemplifies the type of messages I hear most frequently from souls who have crossed:

> It is at once startling and magnificent. I wonder that we slip so easily into our new roles. The splendor far exceeds anything on earth. And yet, the joyous experience of earth sings at a depth that colors our return. Somehow, experiencing both here and there moves us in ways that could not otherwise be accomplished.

Such a report brings exuberance to the heart. Life quickens when we understand death as celebration, death as birth, and death as sacred transformation. Souls who make the effort to communicate after they have crossed over, want very much to allay any fears. They are under no obligation to return, which makes their efforts all the more touching. If there were something foreboding to report, I believe they would try to warn us. One soul, who chose to go through what she called the nine hells, stated that she did so to test herself.

Eternal life from this perspective means that our souls are eternal and can choose to temporarily take physical form. Souls are made of energy. Science tells us that energy cannot be destroyed, only transmuted. Souls can thereby live in the expanded realms and they can change energetically to live within the mortal frame. As multidimensional beings, souls have the capacity to explore many different realms of consciousness, different frequencies, and different states of being. The focus of human form on earth is but one of these choices. And yet, this may be a very limited definition, for one cannot on any level presuppose the Infinite, the All, the Great Spirit, God/Goddess. Just when we begin to think that we somewhat comprehend creation, it changes in a way that stops the mind in its tracks. Defining eternal life as a continuous journey that is forever creating something new out of what currently exists is a good option. I like to call this perspective *ever becoming*. A soul is a work in progress, ever learning and growing spiritually.

It is of note that for every soul return, there is a remembering that takes place. Often souls are aghast that they could have forgotten something so spectacular. Death is frequently an overwhelmingly arduous task primarily because of the belief that the third dimension reigns supreme. Like birth, death brings physiological complexities and discomfort. Knowing that the crossing is a profoundly beautiful moment tempers the experience of discomfort considerably.

An additional encumbrance is the mindset of the Western World of today, which has a largely left-brain orientation. The left-brain cannot understand a mysterious journey like death, just as it cannot comprehend the essence of a painting or a poem. It is from such a limited position that one discards Radiant Beauty as impossible, rendering a very stark reality indeed. Rather than perpetuating something so unworkable, the imperative is for each of us to become conscious so that we each can choose wisely from the soul perspective.

The Great Beyond is magical and mystical. It does not bow to any constricted definition of reality. Souls are most often at home immediately upon remembering the connection. There is a sense of wonder, awe and reverence. There is a sense of benevolence. There is a sense of belonging and being that does not exist on earth. Colors are more varied. Sound is more pure. We, very simply, remember that each of us is each made of that which lies beyond and wonder how it was possible to forget.

In order to give you an understanding of the depth and breadth of soul passage experiences, in the following pages I will share numerous personal accounts. As you read, I hope that what becomes obvious is that one's crossing of the threshold is totally unique to that individual. In reading these personal accounts, please bear in mind that while it would be nice to have sequencing consistent, that is not how things happen in the Expanded World. There is great variation in how the process unfolds and thus, there is great variation in the following descriptions. I am often up in the middle of the night doing this work. It is a dramatic change in consciousness, which does not lend itself to writing down dates and times, although sometimes I am able to do so. I have also attempted to give some factual information to give you a sense of how the process unfolds for a given individual.

Please remember that the information shared by Spirit is just that—it is the information shared. There is no time for me to ask questions. It is an improvisation, requiring full living attention moment by moment. What is abundantly clear and consistent is that we cannot think our way through the dying process. It is not logical. Open hearts are the basis for moving forward with clarity and peace.

I have grouped the soul experiences in three groups in this chapter. The first group contains descriptions of passages with souls who are Ready to Transition. Up to the point of our meeting, they may or may not have had a difficult time. When we meet, these souls are ready to make the transition pretty quickly. The second group contains passages of Souls Needing More Time. In general, these souls are ready but have things to finish or resolve, or simply require a bit more time to get used to the idea of crossing over. The third group consists of souls who are Resisting Crossing Over due to fear, misunderstandings, or not wanting to leave loved-ones. Their questions or needs are an important part of becoming ready to transition, which require time and effort. There is of course overlap with these arbitrary groupings, but in general the division brings more awareness to the actual process of dying.

To honor each soul who has shared a portion of the journey into the Expanded World, each begins on a new page. Please pause for a moment of reflection following each journey or poem.

Souls Ready to Transition

Toby, Donald, Pamela, and Esther were each ready or close to being ready to transition when I met them. Toby just had one question, and when that was answered, she was ready to go. Donald was exhausted on the physical and soul level. This exhaustion left him open to listen to spiritual direction. Pamela made a courageous decision to disconnect life support systems. Esther was ready on every level.

Toby

When I meet Toby in the Subtle Realms, her hair is wild. This is a reflection of her emotional state rather than her personal appearance. Her fingers are long and her nails are beautifully manicured. Our meeting is natural and effortless. She is in Montreal, Canada. I am in Colorado. All of my time with her is in the Expanded Realms in year 2016.

Toby says she is tired of being in the hospital so I invite her soul for a walk. We move out of the hospital and she is thrilled to feel the breeze. Up on the rooftop we create our little sanctuary. Toby is chilly so I put a shawl around her shoulders. When she is comfortable she looks at me and asks, "What will it (death) be like?"

I reply, "Just like this. You will meet other beings. You will see your ancestors."

"You're kidding!"

"No," I reply.

"So, I am not going to die die. I am just going to leave here and go somewhere else."

"Exactly."

"Why don't they tell people these things?"

Toby is silent for a long while. We look at the lights of the city, listen to the hustle and bustle down below, observe the stars (as much as we can see them), and enjoy feeling the night air breeze. It is chilly!

"So, dying isn't dying. Dying is living. How convoluted can a message get? This is unbelievable! When can I go?"

"Whenever you feel ready."

"OK. I just can't believe this. Thank you, Thank you. Thank you. I better go back."

As we are returning to the hospital room, Toby says it feels too hot, almost suffocating. "I don't know how long I can stay here."

I hold the hand of her soul as she climbs into the hospital bed. She repeats, "I am not going to die die. I am just going to go live somewhere else. Unbelievable."

Suddenly, Toby's soul sits up from her body. "I am just too excited to lie here. Let's go!"

Holding soul hands, we start running and move so fast that it becomes a blur. This joyful race continues for quite a while until we come to a place of rolling hills where each of us collapses on the ground laughing, laughing and laughing. The grass-like ground is golden, yet soft, and is clearly living and vibrant. There is great space all around. It is still and silent. We can see the rolling hills continue off in the distance.

Toby finally sits up and asks, "Where are we? This place is magical. Is it real?"

"Yes."

Laughter erupts again. After we have regrouped from our hysterics, we begin slowly walking amongst the hills. It is peaceful, silent, open, welcoming, although we are the only ones around. I notice that Toby's frequency is adjusting beautifully. She is thrilled.

Shortly, out of the corner of my eye, I notice a large, silvery, iridescent bubble touching down by Toby. Out steps a female to welcome her. They embrace affectionately. Clearly they are thrilled to see each other again. Shortly, when we look up, we see hundreds of these magnificent bubbles streaming silently across the brilliant blue sky towards Toby. The enchanting beauty of this scene is astounding. We are speechless. Slowly, the other bubbles touch down one by one. Each ancestor emerges and delightedly hugs Toby until the entire scene becomes a swirl of meeting and greeting, melting, and intermingling color. Tremendous laughter breaks the profound silence.

Donald

Our first connection is a Saturday night. The second is Sunday night. Each time Donald is overwhelmed, exhausted, and unable to have anything required of him. He has been getting used to the idea of leaving the earth plane. All of my time with him is in the Expanded Realms in year 2016.

Early Monday evening Donald is ready to begin walking to the Other Side. As the walk begins, there is an angel on one side of Donald and I am on the other. We are literally holding his soul upright because he is so exhausted. We walk very little…little steps and little distance. Almost immediately we can hear an amazing ancestral choir of all male voices. They sing the following song over and over again as a chant:

> *Donald*
> *Can you hear the song tonight?*
> *Donald*
> *Can you see the Blessed Light?*
>
> *Bless the One*
> *Bless the One*
> *Bless the One*
> *Bless the One*

This singing strengthens Donald's soul and spirit. He is very inspired. There are hundreds of strong, male voices.

We move on a little farther to absolute silence. It is peaceful and meditative with a sense of divine purity. There is a different balance needed to walk this part of the path so we move very slowly. Donald's frequency begins lifting.

Very curiously, we then hear something that sounds like a train moving along the tracks. As it gets louder and louder, almost deafening, it seems to be many trains at once. The angel and I hold Donald steadfastly so he will not be knocked over by the intensity of the sound.

We continue and again reach the beautiful Sacred Silence. Donald breathes in the gentle, rejuvenating quality and relaxes considerably.

Glorious music begins entering and expanding our hearts. Ancestors of an all female choir beckon us forward. Just like the men did, the women repeat the song many times like a chant:

> *Hear thy soul*
> *Whispering*
> *Hear him call your name*
> *Blessed be*
> *Song of Truth*
> *Soon you shall be free.*

The beauty and expansion of our hearts helps Donald stand tall. Although the angel and I are still on either side of him holding his arms, his soul is now walking a stronger walk.

Another short distance finds us in the deep, meditative sacred silence. It is welcomed with open arms. We all walk very slowly.

The quiet has a deeply reflective quality so we are all present with that, and we do not talk.

Quite suddenly, there is an amazingly beautiful scent wafting through the air. It is subtle, delicate, and delicious. There is no name for it on earth. It is calming, welcoming.

On the heels of the extraordinary scent comes a series of words for Donald: *true essence; gentle being; release all cares; feel your Light*. Donald deeply breathes in conscious awareness and becomes one with the words. The three of us are majestically seated in the center of and gently held by, a magnificent lotus blossom. I notice that Donald's frequency is adjusting beautifully. Sipping nectar, we visit quietly within the folds of the radiant flower.

Suddenly, gorgeous celebratory singing erupts. We see that the hundreds of ancestors encircling us are joined by angelic beings, which magnify the sound tremendously. They are completely around us and form what looks like a tulip blossom emerging from the lotus flower. This explosion of joyous singing causes Donald to jump up to give the angel and me a most beautiful hug. We watch mesmerized by the incredible sight before our eyes. The words I remember are:

> *Song so true*
> *Ever loving, ever living in the Light*
> *Song so true*
> *Ever bringing, each the joyous Sight.*

Donald's knowing has returned. He is beaming. He is Home. He will go with the ancestors when the celebration is complete.

Pamela

Pamela has Lou Gehrig's disease. After eight months on life support, she feels ready to release the body to cross the threshold. Pamela sets her departure for a specific date and time. Her friends and family gather. All of my time with her is in the Expanded Realms in year 2013.

My soul connects with Pamela's soul prior to the appointed hour to help allay any fears. She is actually pretty relaxed and clear. As we are preparing, I see an enormous two hundred foot white lily form in the cosmos directly over Pamela's bed. It will serve as her transport to the Great Beyond. When the life support systems are disconnected, Pamela is lifted immediately and gracefully away from the reach of the body up through the center of the lily flower transport. Together, she and I are then seated on a bench in a brilliantly hued garden. Pamela is shaking her head saying *"pshew,"* as if trying to shake out the cobwebs. She is given a drink of Divine Nectar to strengthen her vibration. This is a rapid shift in frequency so Spirit offers every support for her to make the change quickly.

When Pamela gets her bearings, she says, "This is so beautiful!" She gives me a deeply loving hug and says, "Thank you." Pamela glances down at the body, which is within sight, and lets everything go. We then quietly walk on a meandering path to a high waterfall with a grand pool of water at its base. Pamela spontaneously dives in for a swim, ecstatic to be moving again. When she completes her relaxing swim, we begin talking. I tell her that I am a friend of her cousin.

She asks why I am helping her so I describe this work. We spend about an hour of earth time together to allow for her vibration to shift. As Pamela begins feeling more fluid with the frequencies, she notices an enormous swing with a wooden-like seat. She immediately runs to begin joyfully swinging. As she swings, Pamela is beaming with her beautiful smile, which turns to uproarious laughter as she remembers the Cosmic Song. She is amazed that she could have forgotten something so important. Our eyes meet and radiate deep sisterly love for one another.

Pamela and I slowly return to the brilliantly hued garden. The ancestors have been patiently waiting in the distance for Pamela's knowing to return. At the close of our hour together, the ancestors begin streaming into the garden from five directions. They are encircling and embracing Pamela. Her ecstatic joy is definitely contagious. As the celebratory welcome proceeds, I begin backing away knowing that she is in good hands.

Esther

Esther is preparing to transition. Her family feels she is ready and hopes to be able to hear of her journey to the Other Side. All of my time with her is in the Subtle Realms in year 2015.

Esther's journey begins with a dance! Interestingly, many spirit beings join with us in a line dance before moving across the threshold. The rhythm is 1, 2, 3; 1, 2, 3; clap on the second third; repeat; then a crossover double step to the count of 4. The words to accompany are "We're going home today." Esther finds this great fun. The entourage moves across the sky in a line doing this very celebratory song and dance for about ten minutes of earth time.

As we approach the crossing point, Esther and I step forward together holding hands. We then walk softly as if not to disturb the gentle particles under our feet until we come to a fog. As we enter the somewhat foreboding dense fog, Esther exclaims, "Oh my!" We continue for a relatively short time until the fog begins to dissipate. As the fog clears, in the distance we can see a splendid City of Light. We both gasp as we realize this is to be Esther's new home.

The City is situated in a circle with brilliant flower gardens and fountains at its center. There is a spectacular Holy Temple at one point in the circle. From a distance, the City looks like a brilliant pulsing flower. Arriving in the City, we find the paths weaving between and around the structures strewn with delicate rose petals. Every path is lined with souls on either side that welcome Esther. We slowly loop up and down and around the entire city. Everyone is beaming, including the two of us!

When we complete the looping, the beings that welcomed Esther are ready to perform in the center circle. They are sharing their deepest gift and have been preparing together for some time. The first group in the circle includes dancers who create amazing sacred geometric shapes. We are both amazed at the ease with which the dancers flow from one very complex shape to the next. The second group is an orchestra playing musical instruments that we cannot identify. We become one with the notes as the orchestra plays extraordinarily beautiful renditions of pieces that neither one of us have ever heard on earth. The third group includes beings that become flowers of light with brilliant colors we cannot name. Esther and I actually become flowers of light with them, which is an amazing short journey in and of itself. Finally, each light child sounds one note in a fascinating sequence, thereby creating an incredible lyrical song.

At this point, I notice that Esther has not yet recognized anyone and wonder when we might find a familiar face. Suddenly, her ancestors begin streaming out of the Holy Temple. Everyone laughs uproariously because the ancestors have planned this celebration as a surprise. Esther is stunned and thrilled. She joyfully accompanies the ancestors into the Holy Temple for a welcome blessing. As she reemerges into the Circle, I wave a happy good-bye, which she and the ancestors heartily return.

I would like to add that one week prior to Esther's departure, she nearly passed. We walked part way and she stopped. She said she needed to say good-bye in a deep way. We sang together for a long while. The last song we sang was Edelweiss from the Sound of Music. She wanted to bless the land, the children, and life. Tears streamed down our faces as we sang, "Bless my homeland forever."

Souls Needing More Time

Elizabeth, Georgiana, and Corrine each had things to finish prior to leaving the earth plane. Elizabeth wanted to get her "spirit legs" so she could walk with strength to her new destination. Georgiana didn't understand why she had to leave and wished to wait for her daughter. Corrine needed to finish spiritual tasks that brought her here and couldn't feel complete without their finalization. Each of these souls was very receptive to the spiritual task at hand within a relatively short time.

Elizabeth

I walk Elizabeth, my beloved Aunt, across the threshold. It is 1996 and I am in Colorado with my infant daughter and Aunt Liz is in Maryland. When we first meet in expanded consciousness, Aunt Liz says she is not ready, that she would like to get her spirit legs so she can walk of her own volition. I let her know that I will return later. When I next check in, she is sitting on the precipice between worlds simultaneously taking in The Greater All and the wonder of her life. Aunt Liz is very comfortable sitting here with her own deep thoughts. This time is very peaceful and tender. We speak briefly and again agree that I will return later.

When she is ready, Aunt Liz lets me know she has her spirit legs. We share a few brief moments and a deeply loving hug. As we walk, she moves with the strength and clarity that were so characteristic of her life. The path is relatively short and gentle. As with my mother, we come to a deep, thick fog where we can see nothing. We continue walking and listening intently. The Sacred Silence holds us tenderly, engulfing our every cell. Suddenly, the fog opens and my Aunt Liz flies into her mother's arms. We are completely encircled by angels beaming enormous love towards these two reunited souls in the center of the circle. When I depart, I have the impression that all of the angels will stay here beaming love towards these two souls for all eternity if that is what they wish.

Georgiana

Georgiana is in Massachusetts and I am in Colorado. She does not understand why she has to leave and wishes to wait for her daughter who is on her way to say good-bye. All of my time with her is in the Expanded Realms in year 1997.

Throughout Georgiana's process, there is a sense of Spirit scrambling to get her used to the idea of the Spirit World before her body fails. Her mind plays this song over and over:

> *I don't understand the crashing of the sea*
> *Why one has to leave is a mystery to me.*

To assist Georgiana, I offer many prayers and practices. When we meet, she is very clear that she does not like strangers, which includes me. Her original instructions are that I may observe but not interact. I agree to this not knowing if it will ever change. After several days, however, she is much more relaxed and actually holds my hand. At this incredible moment we become all mothers and daughters in the Cosmos. She and I both revel in the exceptional joy of this all-encompassing moment.

A few days later, I check in and find Georgiana as a babe in the arms of Mother Mary. This is an extraordinarily touching moment. I can deeply feel the tenderness in Georgiana with the opening of her heart and the vastness of the Eternal Love of Mother Mary, with whom she has a special bond. Ten days after I first meet Georgiana, I am on the phone when the Holy Spirit arrives. Our home is immediately transformed into an amazing Holy Temple filled with the True Essence. I quickly hang up the phone and go to meditate.

When I connect with Georgiana, we begin a long, slow walk filled with many stairs going up. Georgiana has difficulty walking and is very stooped over. Regardless, she is dedicated with purpose. Midway, we stop to wait for her daughter. Georgiana lies down with her head in my lap. I ask if she would like a pillow but she says there is no need. We experience a long, long wait but finally the energies will pause no more. Like the undertow of the ocean tide, we are pulled forward. We thus continue. Soon we arrive at the precipice between worlds. From this magnificent perch, we see a splendid City of Light. Speechless, we both realize this is to be her new Home.

Only a few moments after arriving at this perch, multitudes of clouds roll in and we are no longer able to see anything. Georgiana suddenly gives me a huge bear hug. Wow! What a fabulous moment. Simultaneously, I hear a voice instructing me not to go any further. I reply, "I can't just leave her here!" Ha! Then I quickly reconsider. I say good-bye to Georgiana and turn to walk slowly down the long, long stairs. As I walk, Georgiana begins to expand until she becomes one with the sky exuding a magnificent Celestial Song in which we are both enveloped. Tears of gratitude and more tears flow for each of us. The unrivaled beauty of Spirit reaches deeply into our hearts.

I receive a call the following morning that Georgiana passed peacefully.

Corrine

Corrine's body has a tumor, which recently increased exponentially in size. She is a special friend and I am saddened to hear this news. My time with her is in person and in the Greater World in year 2012.

June: When we first meet in the Greater World, I am wondering if this is going to be her time or if she is going to work through the health crisis. She asks if I will speak at her memorial service. I am stunned, but understand this is her way of letting me know that she is departing.

July: Corrine and I are sitting at a table in the Greater World. We are having tea and she is crying: crying for lost love; crying for leaving too soon. All the while she is also wondering why she is having a difficult time because we both have been through this process many times in different lives. Our connection is strong; our souls work together. Spirit Sisters help each other always. That is our promise and our pact. We talk about what it is to be human and notice that the feelings that go with this experience are deep indeed. It is not easy to say good-bye to loved ones even with the vast spiritual awareness we share. We also talk of the many times we have helped each other at this juncture and that it is always bittersweet.

My soul then stands and walks over to a huge picture window that is dark and foreboding. I take two ends and flip the window over so that Corrine is looking out at eternity. Shimmering brilliance awakens remembrance of the task at hand. The message is that

Corrine is no longer to be looking at what is past but rather embracing her new life. With that, she smiles her radiant smile and says she is ready to keep her focus.

September 11: I go with a friend to say farewell to Corrine on the physical level. Corrine looks beautiful. She occasionally opens her eyes but does not engage with anyone. The serene setting is entirely befitting of this amazing soul: beautiful multicolored silks are draped at the foot of her bed as well as lovely altar of flowers. She rests in the home of dear friends. Reluctantly, I kiss her good-bye.

September 13: Corrine's soul appears to me in a white dress. Our souls are standing together in the Greater World preparing for her transition. Archangels surround us. I recognize Archangel Azreal and know that Corrine's time is quite near.

September 15: Along with many angelic beings, I am Holding the Presence—a practice that Sri Yogananda shared with me—to assist Corrine. Holding the Presence serves as a container for the entire process of Corrine's journey to the Other Side. It is the guiding tone. This involves holding the awareness of the changes in frequency, which occur at each stage, and helping to align Corrine's frequency accordingly.

We meet in the Greater World. Close in her circle are loved ones and friends who surround her. As we begin to cross, we move through the elemental kingdom with fairies, gnomes, elves, and the spirit of Gaia honoring her. We come to many, many angels all wishing her a beautiful walk. Corrine's task on earth has been to work with the male/female balance through helping to shift templates while bringing in the loving Sacred Feminine. At this moment, she pauses to bring forth her last insight to help Gaia and her people before departing. She has been carrying much for the collective unconscious, which has been difficult for her physical body. Angels remind Corrine that there are no time constraints; she is the designer of this crossing. Quan Yin and Kali are here to help her embrace a new beginning. Butterfly Maiden assures her that this is a birth and to embrace the extraordinary transformation.

Corrine turns to say that she would like me to walk with her. She then states that she is going to take her time to be able to take in every tiny nuance of the profound awareness available during a transition between worlds. We joyfully walk arm in arm on a white carpet stretched laterally across the cosmos. Occasionally, we step up two steps. Corrine greets each and every being welcoming her lining both sides of the carpet. Celebration is in the air with grand music and colorful wildflowers strewn on her path.

After the long, exhilarating walk (three days in earth time), we reach the end of the path, where we encounter the Christ and Mary Magdalene welcoming Corrine together! They gently radiate a deeply precious love. Corrine and I both gasp with amazement as we drink in the profound realization that the efforts of many on both sides of the veil are truly restoring the Sacred Feminine. Corrine turns to me and gives me a very tender hug farewell. On the earth plane, I burst into tears. Corrine joyfully goes with the Christ and Mary Magdalene in a swirl of Great Light.

Souls Resisting Crossing the Threshold

Gabrielle, Gladys, Jerry, Violet, Pricilla, Lisa and Townsend each had specific reasons not to leave and actively tried to prolong their lives here. Each needed assistance in coming to terms with the outstanding issue(s) and wanted to feel complete prior to passing. It is important to remember that all reasons for resisting are valid and this is a deeply personal process. Gabrielle did not wish to leave her children. Gladys did not wish to confront a patriarchal God, who might be as punishing as her abusive husband. Jerry believed in nothing, which impeded his process. Violet was encased in a self-created energy field that blocked her movement. Pricilla wanted to be certain her affairs were in order. Lisa needed to release belief systems that were blocking her spiritual growth. Townsend had no belief system that supported the existence of Spirit.

Gabrielle

Gabrielle has cancer and can no longer stay on the earth plane. She does not wish to depart. In particular, she does not want to leave her children. As a mother of young children, the depth of despair for saying good-bye to them is understandably intense. There is much work in the Expanded Realms to assist her acceptance and perspective of the situation. My time with her is in the Greater World in year 2010.

December 2010: My soul spends a long time with Gabrielle's soul today. This is our third session. She sobs and sobs and sobs in my arms in the Holy Temple in the higher dimensions called La'kina. I focus on Holding the Presence with Gabrielle.

I share Tonglen from the Buddhist tradition. It is very powerful for transmuting deep pain. Kali appears to purify destructive thoughts. Archangel Jophiel works to help Gabrielle see beauty in all its dimensions and forms. Other Light Beings bring gifts to assist Gabrielle in shifting her frequency. I think about the transference of consciousness. Immediately upon the thought, the Christ appears to place the "Ever abiding Peace which passeth all understanding" into her heart. She takes it in deeply. Momentarily, Gabrielle begins connecting with hearts all over the world. It is an ecstatic moment with deep love and brilliance at its core. It is eternal in nature, revealing the caring through all time. When my physical self must depart, Gabrielle is resting peacefully in La'kina, the Holy Temple with many angelic beings watching over her. My soul will stay with her until she passes.

I receive an email that Gabrielle has peacefully passed.

Gladys

In this soul passage experience, Gladys comes to know her Greater Self, her Soul, her true essence or the eternal aspect of self, and resolves the dilemma of not being able to cross the threshold or to stay on the earth plane. We connect through meditation and all of my time with her is in the Expanded Realms in year 1997.

Saturday: I pray for Gladys and place heather in the prayer basket to help her connect with her soul. Although I can feel her presence, it is difficult and feels as if she is heavily sedated.

Sunday: I find Gladys encased in unworthiness, which is extremely dense and thick. This circular encasement looks like a wall resembling the Great Wall of China, immoveable and impenetrable. Gently, I wash her feet, brush her hair, and oil her body. I surround her in beauty by draping her in beautiful cloth, and placing flowers and lighted candles. When I sing, Gladys responds with a feeling of wonder and peaceful joy.

Monday: Gladys says she is afraid to go forward because she is afraid God will be as punishing and mean as her abusive husband. This dichotomy causes a profound conflict in Gladys' psyche and results in her inability to live or to die. I call in Divine Mother and Mary, with whom Gladys has a kinship. To assist in diminishing Gladys' pain, I offer Tonglen, the Buddhist practice of breathing in another's pain and breathing out love.

Thursday: I see Gladys sitting quietly in a chair. She is resting.

Wednesday the following week: In the morning, I see a still bell in an archway, a pause in the process. Gladys is resting. At midnight, surprisingly, Gladys pops in to see me. She is smiling and walking with a walker. I invite her to sit and she does so in a pink chair. Suddenly, she jumps up with glee, arches back, feet doubled up behind her as in a modern dance move. She sits back in the chair and we sacredly touch foreheads. Gladys wants to learn how to do the process of Tonglen because she felt enormous relief when I did so for her. We both share the process of breathing in pain and breathing out love for Jane, a mutual friend. Jane receives the spiritual gift gladly and relaxes considerably. Gladys connects with her mother in the spiritual planes and is very excited to see her. My young daughter cries in the next room on the physical plane. I go to her and Gladys stays with me to help comfort my daughter as she endearingly remembers her own children.

Wednesday the following week: Gladys is still in physical form. We are happy to see each other again. Gladys relaxes. I offer the Melchizedek Prayer, a prayer specifically asking for assistance with the correct frequency for Gladys. Gladys then realizes that she wants to enjoy the love of children before she moves on. She remembers her children, tells me of their lives, and the joy of love they shared. I again offer Tonglen and chanting, and call in Divine Mother. Very quickly, the massive Wall of China that encases Gladys becomes a flower garden—a beautiful, living, vibrant, and colorful garden. I receive a call that Gladys has passed.

Jerry

Jerry is preparing for his soul passage. He is in a nursing facility. My time with him is in person and in the Greater World. When in person, Jerry is very aware and remembers everyone but clearly his body is diminishing. The following snapshots occur in year 2011.

Wednesday morning: I enter meditation to be greeted by my soul and Jerry as well as his beloved dog that preceded him in death. We shall escort him to his new home. What a fabulous reunion they have as the dog licks Jerry's face. Jerry's soul is laughing and laughing and laughing at the licking and at the hilarity of the cosmos. His physical self is not ready to cross just yet and does not yet realize what the soul realizes. My soul is thrilled with this sudden turn of events and honored to do this walk in this way. The heavens are preparing and awaiting Jerry's welcome. My soul and the beloved dog stand in awareness 24/7. It is so very sweet.

Wednesday evening, same day: My soul appears with an enormous feather in hand and I wonder what she is going to be doing. The scene moves quickly and I see that it is a purification ceremony. The beloved dog, Jerry and I are in a very quiet, peaceful setting. I light the sage and am sweeping the body with the feather. Jerry is smiling. I chant the Heart Chant from the Cherokee Tradition:

> *Ah, Ah, Ah*
> *Ah, Ah, Ah, Ah*
> *(Repeat)*

Ah tesh na he, na
Ah tesh na he, na
Ah ni qo qo ne, ah ne qo ne
Tesh na, ha ha
Tesh na, ha ha

This beautiful chant of love for the Great Spirit and all beings brings energy into alignment with deep serenity.

Sunday: Jerry is having a difficult time believing that the Expanded World exists. He consistently states, "I believe in nothing." This makes his transition challenging. On the physical level he is quiet and his body is visibly shrinking. His greatest joy is eating ice cream while visiting with family and friends.

A chant sounds from the Unseen World to help Jerry understand the Spirit Realms. White Eagle appears as well to accompany the chant with a drumbeat for maybe ten minutes of earth time.

One with the heartbeat
One with the purr
One with the breeze that blows through the hair
One with the Great Song

When the beautiful chanting subsides, my soul inquires of Jerry, "Can you hear the dog barking at your side? Can you see the tail wagging? Can you feel the lick to greet you? My soul then creates two message cards. The first card reads: "Ensconced in disbelief," with a big X over the words. The second card reads: "Flying free." These messages are to encourage Jerry to choose the freedom of the Great Beyond over limitation.

Thursday am: Jerry's soul and mine visit his new home so we know where he will be going. There is a little cabin with a front porch, lots of huge rock outcroppings surrounded by forest similar to New Mexico. The beloved dog and Jerry joyfully walk and play. Five communities surround the cabin. These five communities are holding space for a peaceful transition and waiting to welcome Jerry and the beloved dog. Ten communities surround the five; twenty communities surround the ten. Jerry can travel anywhere he likes, I am told.

Shortly, we move into sacred ceremony. Elders from the five communities stand center to welcome Jerry. The communities stand in a circle about an acre in size for the welcoming. I am also told that there is heart resonance with the beings in the communities. There is a peaceful flow to this process that allows for quiet reflection and loving community within the context of Jerry's personal rhythm. As Jerry's heart heals and expands, others know and immediately emerge to greet him. This creates a pulsing similar to a star.

Thursday, pm: Following Jerry's departure, I receive this poem:
> *Jerry of the freedom riders singing his song*
> *Jerry in the Joy and Love all the daylong*
> *Vibrant hues and brilliant stars*
> *Gazing out one sees so far*
>
> *Such a conundrum this cosmos scheme*

Just when one has the thread, it breaks in between
The one holding and all that follows after
Such a feeling of despair and seeming disaster

The trick must be holding strong to the center of the theme
That way one can come and go without creating a seam
Rest is good; rest is fine
Oh my heart does feel sublime
Thank you for the wonderful signs.

Violet

Violet is having a difficult time passing to the next realm. Her birth family on earth wishes she would stay on the earth plane and hopes to learn that she is doing just that. All of my time with her is in the Expanded World in year 2014.

Saturday, May 26: When my soul finds Violet, she is completely encased in a dark egg shape. She is scared and calling for her mother in a small child's voice. Violet has created this enclosure to protect herself from difficult circumstances. Yet, by sealing herself off, she also cannot feel love. I call Archangel Azreal, Archangel Sandalphon, Archangel Gabrielle, Archangel Jophiel, Violet's mother, and her son-in-law who are in the Spirit World. All of these beings encircle the egg shape, are Holding the Presence and are sending enormous love day and night.

Sunday, May 27: Violet looks at me and says, "Don't you have something you need to do?" She is accustomed to living with one who works full time so she is stunned that I can be with her for as long as she likes. "I am here to help you. There is no hurry. Just keep taking in the Love."

My soul touches the dark egg shape hoping to energetically help the process along and it turns pink in color. It softens and the color spreads out beyond the dark shape transforming it. This means that Violet is taking in all of the Love being sent to her. She is softening. I am thrilled at her progress.

Violet tells me that she can never again be without Love. She can now only exist in the space that is Love. This is the Love of Spirit. She says, "I have allowed myself to be deceived in this life."

Later in the day: Violet catches a glimpse of her mother in the Spirit World. She is afraid it is a trick. I assure her that it is not a trick. She says she does not know whom to trust. I tell her that some people equate love with ownership and while they try to do the right thing, from such a perspective it is not possible to transmit true love. Also, I tell her that she can trust all of the beings gathered here meaning the angels, her mom, her son-in-law, and me. We are gathered in the Spirit World specifically to help her.

Violet says she keeps trying to figure out what she has done wrong in her life and why she is being punished. I tell her she has done nothing wrong. We also talk about the idea of being able to stay in the body if she can feel the Love of Spirit. It is an option. Whatever changes are necessary can be accomplished for her to feel she is in the right place. She does not have to go to the Other Side if that is the only reason she is leaving. She says she will think about it. If she does decide to go to the Other Side, all of the beings in her circle know the way. She can pick one of us or all can go together. It is her choice.

Sunday night: Violet comes to me to state simply but firmly that she is going to go through the nine hells. I am shocked for I know nothing of the nine hells. My soul tells her, "That is not required of you." Violet says that she knows, but she is going to do so anyway. She should not go alone so my soul will go with her. Violet is pleased.

We spend much of Sunday night moving through the nine hells. Although the journey is arduous, Violet consistently makes wise choices and loving decisions in the midst of great peril. I am so inspired by her. This is her journey so she must make the decisions. I cannot interfere. If something goes wrong, I can help free her but that is my only task.

We go from realm to realm, which is at times totally overwhelming and exhausting. Yet, Violet triumphs each time. What an amazing soul. As we come out of the last realm, we see the angels, her mom, and son-in-law waiting for us and they are beaming! Spirit does not wish for me to recollect the experiences so the memory is erased.

Violet is free. She can now see clearly in the Expanded World so she is thrilled. She is at home in the Love for which she yearned. My alarm sounds. I must go to work.

Monday evening: Violet tells me that she is complete. She is never again going to be deceived. She went through the nine hells to remember the ways and the faces of those she cannot trust. Now, she can take her place with honor among those she can trust. She smiles a beautiful smile at the angels, her mom, her son-in-law, and me. We all return that beautiful joy. I learn Tuesday morning that Violet passed peacefully Monday evening.

Wednesday morning: Violet returns to say thank you bearing the angel wings that she earned.

Lisa

Lisa has been in hospice for eight or nine months when I receive a call. Physicians are astounded that she is still alive since her entire body is riddled with cancer. She is racked with pain and can only get relief with psychotropic drugs, if that. I am asked to check to see what may be holding her here. Clearly she does not wish to leave her husband and children, but there may be something more. She is in Montreal, Canada; I am in Colorado. All of my time with her is in the Expanded Realms in year 2015.

19 September: I find that Lisa is caught under an avalanche of pain and dark. This place is dank and cold with a hard surface like cement. The only glimmer of warmth for Lisa comes from the people around her. She can either be with these people or be with the pain, dark and cold. With only these two choices, she fights with all of her will and strength to stay on the third dimension to be with the people. The either/or has become a self-perpetuating feedback loop.

When I meet her, Spirit shows her a third option. Angelic beings surround her and pour Light, Love and Warmth to nourish and uplift her. She can hear the Great Song, feel the warmth and feel the living Joy of Spirit. I hear that when she crosses, she will cross as Lady Lisa. I see that she will be dressed in a beautiful long white gown. She is stately and lovely. As she places her attention on the beauty, the warmth will release her soul. Such a beautiful being. My soul and the angels will stay with her until she crosses.

October: Lisa and I have been working on finding some measure of meaning in the excruciating situation. I share with her the Buddhist prayer: "May this pain suffice for all sentient beings." She likes that and repeats it over and over as a mantra. She would never want anyone to have to go through the type of pain she has suffered. I also share Tonglen to help reduce the pain. Over time the pain begins to recede and the Love grows exponentially. Lady Lisa feels it and begins to relax.

October 11: A fragmented aspect of Lisa appears at the bottom of a dry well. A child of two or three, she is scared. I take her into my arms for comfort. I also see flags of red, white and green placed outside the palace as a sign of welcome. Her ancestors are preparing for her homecoming.

October 12: Today the fragmented self again presents herself. She shares that she is too scared to cross the threshold. As a small child, she can be in my arms when the crossing occurs, so that becomes the plan. I explain to her that she will be safely on the Other Side before any more changes occur. What a beautiful, heartfelt relief, opens in her.

Monday: I see Lady Lisa in the clouds beaming a gorgeous smile to me.

Tuesday: Angelic beings place Lady Lisa in a golden pond of water to relax her and to intensify the new, very loving frequencies, so she cannot ignore them. They continue to pour Loving Light into the situation and to Lady Lisa.

Wednesday: Lady Lisa and I are outside under the stars. We both see the stars move in a certain configuration as if saluting her. She asks, "Is that for me?" When I say yes, she is totally humbled and honored.

The scene changes and we begin walking in the forest with fallen leaves in the full moonlight. Lisa yearns to remember the unique sound of the crunching of the leaves under her feet. She also etches in her memory the deep musky smell in the air.

The scene shifts again. We find ourselves on the sandy beach listening to the roar of the ocean, smelling the salty water, and feeling the gentle ocean breeze in the full moon. It is a magical night. Lisa and I stand in silent reverie, taking in the glorious experience for a long while. She then spontaneously kneels down to kiss the earth farewell. This is a deeply moving moment. She is preparing to go Home.

Thursday and Friday: We sit together in quiet meditation on the beach.

Saturday night, end of October: We talk about the transitioning process. She feels a wave of relief when I tell her that her soul will arrive home first, and then the body will stop breathing.

Saturday, November 7: I connect with the soul of Lisa. She is very concerned about the person continuing to be in unbearable pain. We discuss the fact that once she withdraws from the body, the suffering stops. The soul realizes that the person is like a wild animal that cannot grow and learn. It is not a good situation.

We move to a temporary place in consciousness to adjust the vibration. Lisa's soul swims in many pools of water with extraordinary waterfalls. There are long stretches of pure white sandy beaches. We walk and talk deeply. Finally, she says she is ready to withdraw from the body and return Home.

Lady Lisa dresses in her long white gown. A white, lacy, delicately formed, flowered shawl is placed around her shoulders. It reaches to the floor in the front; not in the back. She wears a white lily in her hair on the right side. Three delicately formed ankle bracelets adorn her left ankle. She has bare feet.

At one point, Lisa feels a bit nervous and fingers her shawl. A gentleman from the earth plane asks her to dance. This is likely her husband. She declines. This is her final decision to depart. I take her arm and we step onto a simple, narrow path together. The fragmented self is in my arms. Many angels join us part way but Lisa cannot yet see them. We enter a long archway formed by elaborately entwined tree branches from stately trees on either side. Brilliant Light pours through the branches casting radiance and gentle peace as we walk. When we emerge from this long archway, enormous white clouds billow all around with a sun rising straight in front of us. The sight is dazzling and takes our breath away. There are flowers as far as we can see. Lisa asks to stop to take it all in. There is no more fragmented self. Lisa is beautifully whole. She gives me a long and deeply appreciative hug.

In the distance amongst the clouds, we see a castle tower and begin walking towards it. As we draw close, there are many souls lining the path on either side. They kneel as Lady Lisa passes by them. Celebration fills the air. As we step into the castle, straight ahead stands a tall, white bearded, crowned king awaiting her. He is a father figure, not a husband. Tears form in his eyes. Lady Lisa returns to court as a daughter. Attendants appear to attach a long cape at her shoulders, which hangs to the floor in the back with a short train.

Lady Lisa proudly walks forward to take the arm of the King. They take a few steps together. Suddenly, she stops, turns, and runs back to me. She places a long, silver ring on my right index finger as a thank you. It is engraved with something like a flower of life symbol. Tears grip both of us—in the Expanded World and in Colorado where I am sitting. We are sisters through all time. Glimpses of her life in this next world reveal laughing with ancestors and singing with children. She returns to the waiting King and I depart.

Townsend

Townsend does not wish to depart from the earth plane. His time is near and he is no closer to comprehending the spirit world. All of my time with him is in the Expanded Realms in year 2016.

When I find Townsend, his soul is expanding. He has hit the ceiling with the back of his neck and is floating looking down. He feels trapped. He is scared. Also, he is very nervous. As I take his hands and look into his eyes, I say, "I know you don't believe in anything but I am asking that you believe in me and that you trust me."

We gently move down a bit so we can sit across from each other. We don't talk because he is too nervous so I continue sending him deep love. After a time, he finally agrees that he will walk with me. Archangel Azreal is present and holds him on the other arm. We walk slowly together.

We arrive at a resting spot with a small bench and Archangel Azreal and I help Townsend sit down. I bring him nectar to drink, which helps calm him considerably. Townsend dips his toes into the water of a quiet stream. I notice his frequency is improving. Townsend looks at me as says, "This is very beautiful."

I then ask Townsend, "Is there anyone you would like to see?"

He replies, "Yes, my dog." Soon, the dog on the Other Side to which he refers bounds forth to greet his dear master. Townsend is stunned to silence. He looks at me with steady eyes. The sweet dog with long dark hair happily visits with Townsend and then comes over to say hello to me.

A very deep wilderness with extraordinarily tall trees invites our presence. We respond by beginning a beautiful walk into her depths. The silence is profound. The experience of this walk with Townsend, the beloved dog, Archangel Azreal and me in the midst of the Great Forest is deeply touching to my heart. Since it is a very unlikely crew to be walking together, I think of the Wizard of Oz when Dorothy, Tin Man, Scarecrow, and Lion are walking on the Yellow Brick Road.

We come to another resting spot where we help Townsend gently sit on a simple bench. From the silence of the dark green forest, a small child and a woman emerge to greet us. I do not know who they are but they all recognize one another. The child asks Townsend to sit on the ground to play some sort of game with marbles. Townsend laughs as he slides to the ground to play the game. He relaxes considerably and his frequency improves much more.

Soon, Townsend's brother and wife emerge from the deep forest to greet Townsend. Now he is really speechless. He jumps up to run to give them a hearty hug. The knowing has been returning bit by bit. This heartfelt moment etches itself in all of our memories. We sense the gentle love between them.

This is a beautiful reunion in an unusual way. I helped Townsend's sister-in-law and brother very recently with a soul crossing. They are delighted to see me again and come over to give me a thank you hug. They also wish for their daughter to know, "She is an amazing woman." They ask that I share this with her to carry in her heart each day until they meet again.

I introduce everyone to Archangel Azreal. Townsend's knowing has now fully returned and he can see the Archangel. He looks at Archangel Azreal and states unequivocally, "I will forever believe in you."

We all enjoy this reunion on many levels. It is quiet and peaceful. When it is time to go, Townsend takes my hands, looks into my eyes and says, "I don't know how to thank you." He gives me a kiss on the cheek as we bid farewell. He then goes with his brother, sister-in-law, and beloved dog.

Pricilla

The preparation for this death passage lasts for many months—June through November. Pricilla does not wish to leave according to her family. She has cancer and there are no options. Since her entire account is too long to include here, I share snapshots. All of my time with her is in the Expanded Realms in year 2010.

The month of June
Monday: In an afternoon meditation I meet Pricilla. It is peaceful and quiet. We sit and swing on a front porch. I am holding her hand. She does not want to talk. We swing a lot, laugh and feel the coolness in the air. When she is ready to depart, we sacredly touch foreheads as our farewell.

Wednesday morning: Pricilla arrives in my meditation suddenly. She has short white hair and walks with her cane. She sets the cane to the side before sitting on the double white swing on the same porch.

"Everyone feels this way when they are called," I assure her.

"They do!!!!" Pricilla exclaims.

Eternal life is true. The Christ shared this teaching. Your soul has much to do and much to love. You can watch over your family from here. You will see them again when they cross over and you welcome each one. You can send messages from here and so can they. You can send love and so can they. The relationship is different but it is still ongoing if that is what you all would like.

We sit quietly, feeling the breeze and listening to the birds. Pricilla stands up with her cane and says, "That is enough for now." We hold both hands together and look deeply into each other's eyes, sacredly touch foreheads, and she departs. I am still on the swing when she leaves.

Wednesday pm: We meet sitting on the swing on the front porch. Pricilla again sets her cane to the side. She tells me that there is so much to do before she leaves. She also shares that she is afraid there is going to be bickering in the family. Pricilla wishes to help smooth the way for her family.

Spirit sends a message to Pricilla in this meditation: You are a precious jewel and you bring that to be with God. Like ligure, the precious stone in ancient Israel, all souls are precious and rare.

The month of July

I pray for three souls in my evening meditation. We are gathered in the Holy Temple, Oming, awaiting the arrival of another soul when Pricilla arrives with her cane. Pricilla is happy to lie on the sacred bed in the Temple. Archangel Michael cuts cords to the third dimension. Archangel Raphael is present to help heal wounds so Pricilla can move on. Archangel Jophiel is helping her to see the great beauty and go towards it. Archangel Gabrielle is helping with communication with Pricilla's family.

The month of August
Again I pray for the three souls having difficulty leaving the third dimension. I am immediately transported to the Holy Temple where many spiritual beings are gathered, although I cannot tell who they are. Pricilla is second to lie in the healing bed. I hold her hand and listen intently to her story. Spirit opens the heavens and gives her a mega dose of universal awareness. This brings to light the nanosecond that will pass between her departing and her seeing her family again. All three souls are told that Eternal Life is real and that the body is only temporary.

We move to the floor where each soul sits in a chair. Together we practice merging into an etheric flower and then separating out three times. I then take three stones from my pouch and give them each one. This is to help them all have something tangible to hold on to from one world to the next. They each become radiant when holding these stones in their palms. We bow to each other and the session is over.

The month of September
Pricilla is steadfastly working on family matters during this time.

The month of October
I am in meditation when I receive this song for Pricilla. Hundreds of ancestors are gathered to sing. This is an incredible sight and the deep caring through all time is profoundly apparent.

Oh Pricilla, can you hear us calling you?
Oh Pricilla, we await your sound so true.
Can you hear us?
Can you focus on the Light?
We're here for you to welcome you to gain your truest sight.

As you're walking, notice each and every sound
As you're walking, everything will seem profound.
Keep your focus on the Light and on God's Grace
Then you will move with assurance to your brand new space.

Oh Pricilla, There are wonders waiting here
Oh Pricilla, There is nothing you must fear.
Have an open heart, let the Christ be your guide
You will see his Radiance Pure as a beacon in the sky.

The Light within, the Light without will merge into One.
The Joy within, the Joy without will vibrate like the sun.
Let your cares go, they need not come along
What serves you now is staying true to the One Great Song.

Oh Pricilla, the love you seek is here
Oh Pricilla, the Truth will help you steer
Your might ship, the voyage long.
The Essence of the Might Gong will vibrate true to carry you along.

The thunderous waves will lap at your door
The stormy seas will pound at the floor.
Don't let them in, hold your faith so dear
This will keep you from an overwhelming fear.

Then ..... The Peace ..... arrives
For that, do strive.
We will be there to greet you, sweet one on high.

Mid October

The ancestors have been singing continuously as if to infuse Pricilla with the frequency that is not to be hers. I see Pricilla as a babe lying very still and listening intently to everything being sung and said. I approach her gently and sing of my admiration for her incredible courage, the love of the angels, the Christ, and the Divine Mother. She continues to be very, very still. The universe at large is waiting with great anticipation.

Pricilla is resting in the womb of the Great Mother, while the muted stars as candles light the way and one brilliant star appears to hold the focus. Beings gathered at the Holy Temple are holding the vibration: Sri Yogananda, angelic presences, and my soul. We are hushed, awaiting the birth, Holding the Presence. A blossom could burst forth at any moment. *Ommming* is constant as well as the singing of the ancestral choir. This is extraordinarily beautiful.

Angels share what they are seeing:

Archangel Azreal sees a solid footprint, as if Pricilla has left a deep imprint for all to see and understand.

Archangel Gabrielle notices all of the people working together to assist the process.

Quan Yin sees vibrations of music rising towards the higher spheres, which is a precursor of a birth into the heavens.

Butterfly Maiden sees a cocoon throbbing as if ready to burst.

Dana notices flowers beginning to grow roots and reaching out.

Sri Yogananda sees the majesty of the Great All, the Divine Symphony, the utter breathless beauty.

Sush Al'Mundra sees spirit sisters working joyfully to assist this sacred endeavor.

Friday: I connect with Pricilla in my evening meditation. The following information is in response to her questions, which are too numerous to include here.

It seems like you want this to make sense. It does not make sense to the mind. This is a creative universe. Something new is constantly being birthed and what is no longer needed falls away. This includes bodies when they are no longer able to work well.

What you are experiencing is not death actually but change. It—expanded consciousness—is like prisms changing color. The changes are the dance, the Great Song singing through you, and the Living Essence growing, blossoming, fading; growing, blossoming, fading. That is the rhythm of the Song. It all feels glorious and perfectly natural. It feels like waking from a dream. It is a gift, a beautiful gift from the Absolute.

Can you see your ancestors? Yes. They will show you what you need to know. Can you feel the words vibrating in the air?

Your soul is the true, the eternal you, the vast you. The mind is an instrument to help you complete your tasks on earth. It has very specific, limited duties. When your focus again becomes the soul, all divine qualities flow through you without obstruction. There is a knowing that propels action. It is easier to understand the interconnectedness of all things: stars, planets, souls, flowers, and songs.

Month of November
Sunday: Pricilla feels trapped and cannot get out of the body. She is trying to use will and it does not work. Will is what has kept her alive and allowed her to finish her earthly tasks.

Wednesday: Pricilla arrives very tired. We go to the Holy Temple. I am holding her hand and singing to her when a golden bird appears as a gift from Spirit. This little bird is singing while perched with the little head rubbing against her neck and jaw. *Ommming* is constant. It becomes very peaceful. There is much singing and encouragement for Pricilla to love the little bird, sing her song and feel the joy. Then there is peaceful silence.

Later in November
Friday: We are immersed in ceremony. Pricilla is walking with someone on either side of her. Rose petals are strewn on the path. She is wearing a long dress, almost Hawiian in nature, green with white flowers. There are lots of brilliantly hued flowers everywhere. Her ancestors line the path on either side. She joyously greets each one.

The Christ appears blessing all, over all. Pricilla and I walk up an incline where we see a door. We go through this door together. It is cold, foggy and becomes inky dark, still and silent. We are the only things moving. As we emerge from the inky dark, Pricilla is wearing a long white dress. We come to a valley with a long winding river. There is a Holy Temple up a short hill with a winding path to get to it. Bach's "Jesu Joy of Man's Desiring" is sounding along with the sound of *Om* and the singing of the ancestors. Bells are ringing and great angelic music fills the air. Pricilla greets each soul along the path. When we arrive at the Holy Temple, it is time for me to depart.

The month of December
I settle into meditation and call to Pricilla. She emerges to greet me. We join hands and look deeply into each other's universal eyes, where we see worlds beyond worlds. She grows as large as the sky and returns to herself. I grow as large as the sky and return to myself. We both grow as large as the sky together and return with gales of laughter. We sacredly touch foreheads, have a deep embrace, and part ways.

Gleaning Understanding

Each of the foregoing examples is a powerful statement of sacred birth into the next realm. Each is inspiring in its own way. I never know what is exactly going to transpire, and yet, I rest in the Heart of the Divine ever knowing that all is perfect. My soul is fluid in the next world. As a soul infused with oneness of Spirit, in service to the Divine Plan, I do not have to wonder if she will figure it out. Spirit is always present and available. One thought brings reinforcements. Also, there are times when Spirit brings answers before I ask. There is such a beautiful sense of benevolence throughout the Great Beyond. I cannot overemphasize this point.

Every soul has a special significance in the Great Heart. While it may not seem so on this earth plane, the tender thoughtfulness of Spirit during a soul passage continues to astound me. It is we who have forgotten how to work with Spirit. This is something that can be remembered at any time. Yet, if one does not do so in the process of life, it will be done at the time of transitioning to the next realm. Assisting a loved one or other during a transition offers the supreme opportunities to honor that soul as well as to remember things we have forgotten. Do not let the inspiration pass by unseized.

Insights for Those Preparing to Cross Over:
- I consistently have positive experiences in the next world.
- One can be reunited with pets and/or loved ones if that is what one wishes.
- The Great Beyond is magical and mystical, not linear.
- The process of crossing the threshold is deeply engaging moment by moment.
- Pay attention.
- Invite Spirit to assist.

- Souls sometimes choose difficult tasks, such as self-tests.
- Will impedes the process of crossing over. Merging is a more accurate description of what occurs.
- Angels and archangels are not bound by any religion. Call on them freely.
- Listen and watch for ancestors and others to share messages through visions, poetry, or song.
- Value your own experience. There are many worlds in the Cosmos.

Insights for Families and Professionals:
- While assisting someone who is crossing the threshold, remember that each of us has an eternal aspect, core essence, or soul.
- Souls interpret things differently than people do.
- We do not always know with whom we are walking on earth. Souls take on challenges for the collective experience, and may appear less powerful on earth.
- Focusing only on the fading body brings solely grief and pain. Focusing on greeting the emerging soul offers the possibility of witnessing sacred celebration.
- Change in perception is one way that the left brain can understand what it means to have a change in consciousness. Thus, it calms in the face of perceived calamity.

- The natural order is for a family member to accompany a loved one across the threshold. Conscious awareness allows this beautiful expression to emerge.
- Singing is a key that carries the love, holds the vibrational connection, helps to guide the way, and unlocks the door in the heart.
- Commitment to holding the focus for the higher awareness is a necessary component.
- Families, professionals, and Soul Passage Midwives can each help allay fears, provide insight, and ease the way for loved ones who are crossing the threshold.

Conclusion

When in the presence of such amazing personal accounts, it is almost shocking that familiarity is an overriding experience. That alone tells us that something is amiss with the current understandings and interpretations of death and soul passage. Growing in awareness of the soul, core essence, and the Higher Realms is a sacred endeavor of remembering, which can help each and every one of us.

You are both yourself and your archetype, the extended, godded self, residing in the archetypal realm. Thus, a part of us resides in the archetypal realm that transcends time and space and a part of us dwells her in existential time and space. In the "mysteries," the initiates grew into awareness of their double nature.

Jean Houston, (*The Search for the Beloved*)

Chapter Three
Souls Who Have Crossed the Threshold

I feel it is important to hear from souls who have crossed the threshold. When my mother returned to say thank you, any tendency to discount the experience totally dissolved. Souls often return to say thank you for the assistance during their passages. Nothing could be more deeply meaningful. Jerry shared his poem with insights about soul passage and thanked me for the assistance; Violet returned to say thank you with her angel wings. Both of my parents returned to say thank you following their passages to let me know that they were fine. The actions of these souls continue the weaving of worlds with a higher level of communication.

In this chapter, souls from the Other Side share insights. These are beautiful gifts to be treasured. Paul, Sunaya, Andrew, Gini, Dan, James, and Michael all have important information to share with the world. Their respective journeys encompass a difficulty to overcome or a desire to let humanity know that there is nothing to fear on the Other Side. They are under no obligation to return and it takes an enormous effort on their part to do so. These messages are received after the crossing of each soul.

Paul

Paul's soul passage message is for parents everywhere who have lost children early in life. Paul, a young boy of eight years from Kentucky, died in a car accident several weeks prior to my receiving a call. My time with him is in the Subtle Realms in year 2015.

When I connect with Paul's soul, he visually shows me what happened at the time of the impact. An enormous hand reached down and pulled him up away from the wreckage. It was quick and decisive. He felt no pain. On the Other Side, he found himself in the arms of a much-loved grandpa. He very much remembered walking and holding hands with this larger-than-life figure when he was just a toddler. The picture in his mind of them together was clear and deeply touching. Their reunion was a surprise and a celebration of familiar love. He felt great joy at being with this blessed person. Paul also wanted me to know that the transition process was very easy and natural.

Paul's message is simple. He deeply yearns for his parents to know this story: He is happy; his transition was easy; he will see his parents again. Unfortunately, his parents cannot hear his message because they are lost in their grief. He hopes that someday they will understand. Paul also hopes that parents of other children who cross over will open their hearts to his message.

Sunaya

Suicide presents a very delicate situation. And yet, the love and considerable thoughtfulness of Source allows for delicate change. The depth of caring of Spirit is very apparent in this poem, which I receive one week following the soul passage. I do not know until after I receive the poem that this is a teen suicide in year 2009.

Sunaya with LOVE holding

Stillness in the night

Realigning, soft sounds of comfort

Angelic cocoon surrounding her light

Dim and confused, relaxing day by day

Process unfolding, moving in little ways

    Growing

        Like a babe,

            In the Mother's Womb.

Andrew

A friend calls regarding a friend of his from Texas who has suddenly died of a heart attack. Very recently, he had told this friend, Andrew, about Soul Passage Midwifery and shared my name. Andrew was a bit skeptical but happy to consider that it might be true. His sudden death brings us face to face. All of my time with Andrew is in the Great Beyond in year 2014.

When my soul finds Andrew's soul, he is running in desert sand and has been running for nearly two days of earth time. He is exhausted. I get his attention and help him to slow down. When I inquire of his destination, he points to the mountain range off in the distance. He is trying to get home, which he perceives to be in the distant mountains.

I invite him to sit down for tea and a rest. He accepts. I make a fire to help warm us both as well as prepare the tea. As we are sipping tea, several angels join us. Andrew cannot see them but he continues to be able to see me. When his frequency changes, he will be able to see the angels as well.

Andrew tells me that he can't understand what has happened to him. "It shouldn't be so difficult to get home," he explains. He has been running but doesn't seem to be any closer to the mountains. I listen quietly until he has finished the full description of his circumstances.

When he has finished, I explain that he has crossed the threshold. He finds this very difficult to believe and states that it cannot be so. I ask him if he remembers the conversation with his friend about soul work with people crossing the threshold. "Yes, very much so." He says he is interested in learning more about that work. I then state that I am that person/soul to which his friend was referring. He is shocked and does a double take. After several minutes, he looks at me very directly while it dawns on him that what I am saying is true. The conversation he had with his friend just a week or two ago is pivotal in his being able to understand and accept his circumstances. We continue talking until his frequency has fully adjusted and his knowing has returned.

When this process is complete, he can see and is ready to go with the angelic beings that have been patiently waiting. He shares a very grateful thank you. We have a gentle farewell.

Gini

Following the crossing of an elder at the Anam Chara Home in Boulder, Colorado, I received this beautiful poem. Gini had lived at Anam Chara for two years. She had crossed earlier in the day in August of year 2010.

> *Gini, with PEACE, with LOVE holding*
> *The Flame from the Throne above*
> *Old friends, new friends, families of Light*
> *She flew into hands with absolute delight*
>
> *Storms past, remembered no more*
> *Gracefully moved through the Door*
> *Of Eternal Life, the coveted realm*
> *No need for tears, no need to dwell*
> *In the land of sorrows, as if she fell*
>
> *She sends her love, appreciation and praises*
> *To Anam Chara staff with joy that blazes*
> *A path for others to follow true*
> *It is set with intention and holds like glue*
>
> *Follow the course; be bold and strong*
> *Nothing can stop the amazing True Song*
> *For family, friends and all gifts shared*
> *Live life to the fullest, live life with flair*
> *Bring each experience as deep as you dare*
>
> *The caring endures, the praises sing*
> *The joy unbounded flies with wings*
> *Into the Heart of the Beloved so Pure*
> *Filled with Celebration, always to endure*
>
> *My song has been sung*
>   *My heart has been full*
>   *My love for each never a blur*

I hold out my hand with pure delight
    To share with others keen insight

Waste no time, tarry not at the helm
Take charge to create the new Loving Realm
A bouquet of experiences I carry with me
My song I send to say I am free.

Dan

Dan is aging and does not wish to go through the humiliation of physically declining. He hangs himself in a public place. My time with him is in the Greater World in year 2010.

When my soul meets Dan's soul in the Greater World, he is filled with such intense remorse that no one can get near him. He is like a severely wounded wild animal. Every being must keep its distance or reap its peril. He is in a bare, square, boxlike structure. My soul touches in extremely lightly to keep track of his minute progress throughout the day, awaiting an opportunity to get closer.

After approximately six hours of earth time, my soul is able to sit beside him. We say nothing. I sit for a seemingly long time continuously sending him deep love along with many angelic beings. Eventually, I begin quietly talking with him. Dan and I are completely encircled by many light beings who hold us in eternal awareness, and help the frequency to lift. After a time, I am able to gently put my arm around him. We continue to sit in silence for a long while breathing in the nectar of profound love. When he is finally able to stand, I quietly escort him to the angelic presences that help provide care for such fractured beings.

James

I am meditating in my bedroom when James, my older brother, suddenly appears in spirit form. Physically, we are miles apart. He is in Maryland. I am in Colorado. It is a warm Friday night in August. All of my time with him is in the Subtle Realms in year 1997.

The ghastly appearance of the ultra sickened colors of brown, black, putrid green and yellow in his spirit squeezes the life out of me. He stands in front of me saying nothing. I am in a panic, knowing it is a call for help but not knowing what to do. Emotionally devastated and drained of all life, I feel I can do nothing.

Saturday morning I contact a friend in Maryland and we begin trying to find James. No one knows where he is nor has anyone seen him in quite some time. His children have not seen him. Finally, on Monday morning, I call a hospital nearby his home. The nurse tells me that he "expired" on Sunday night.

James had been intent on drinking himself to death in spite of all the friends and family who tried to help him see otherwise. We all wished we could find a way to relieve his intense suffering. Many detoxification treatments later, we continued to cling to hope for a miracle. He could have died on the streets and we would never have known. His last moments were in a hospital where people were caring for him. That was the miracle.

One month following his crossing, my heart yearns to know how he is doing. When I find James, he does not wish to speak. I see him in a wheelchair with loving spirit beings surrounding him. Thus, I know he is receiving the help he needs and feel grateful. Quietly, I depart.

Years later I come to understand that my soul helped James. That is her mission. Whether I, Patricia, am aware or not, my soul continues her work. She helped him to get to the angelic beings that could assist him.

In January of 2011, James, once again, appears in spirit form. He is bright and clear with an electrifying spirit. At this moment, he is with his divine feminine complement, I am told. Whole and happy, he returns to say thank you and to encourage me to share his story.

Michael

Following the passing of Michael, I receive this poem from his soul in year 2013.

*I send love and butterfly kissings
To those for whom it seems I am missing*

    *All I ask of you is
Forever to remember me
As loving you*

*The truth of Love in Eternal Way
Blazes through us each and every day
How we don't notice is shocking almost
Living life only as a piece of toast
Burned as charcoal from heating too long
Instead of embracing the Beautiful Song*

*Ever flowing, ever piercing the end of death's door
To kindred spirits, remember the store
Containing a thousand wishes, ours for the making
Rather than emptiness, ours for the taking*

*Enchanting, beguiling, the illusion begs on
Yet, we can awaken in a moment, to don
The gilded robes of Awareness and Joy
Laid neatly, so neatly, beside the toys*

*I harken you my friends
This experience now, to lighten and bend
Your focus in a new direction for good
Embracing Divine Love where I once stood
We shall sing and dance and laugh once more
Because there is naught such a thing as death's door
To my wife, my family, my friends, horses too
Know only that I love you and love is the glue.*

Gleaning Understanding:

Moving more deeply into the Expanded World is exciting and interesting! Souls are not arbitrarily assigned boring tasks. They are, in fact, the makers of their experiences through wishing to serve, to accomplish, to learn, to grow, and to expand to the next level. Beings of Light are ever present with assisting all efforts at the time of a soul passage as well as in the After Life.

Insights for Those Preparing to Cross Over:

- Souls who return bring beautifully positive messages about the After Life.
- Children are cared for in a deeply loving way on the Other Side.
- Sudden death can bring challenges in understanding where one is. Angels are ever present with such situations.
- Think about what your belief systems are concerning the After Life.

Insights for Families and Professionals:

- Souls who have gotten lost on earth are rehabilitated in the Higher Realms.
- Life on earth and life in the Expanded Realms have things in common.
- Children who cross over have insights to share with parents and others.

Conclusion

Learning about conscious death passage is an intriguing and fascinating topic. This is a facet of our eternal growth, which can bring much love and endearment. Taking the time to explore the Expanded Realms at the time of death brings answers for which we have yearned. Seemingly obscure secrets are standing in the wings awaiting our inquiry. Death is not something we don't want to do; it is a passage, which we do want to make. It is not the end. It is the next step. It is, indeed, a beginning, a birth.

Part II:

Opening to Soul Passage Midwifery

Part II:
Introduction

Soul Passage Midwifery can be a calling or one can choose to share this skill within the context of the family setting to help loved ones through their passages. Since you are working on a soul level, you can choose to be present in person or to work long distance.

To be present with someone who is crossing the threshold requires an expansion of consciousness or seeing through different eyes. The chapters in this section speak to the essence of this process, which I have experienced many times. In actuality, the process is quite simple but using words to explain it feels cumbersome, like putting the Cosmos in a thimble. As essential guides along the way, wise words from archangels help inform this process. Sri Yogananda offers a technique to secure the appropriate frequency or tone for the journey. It is my hope that practicing the perspectives presented will help those of you who are interested to come into alignment with and open to this beautiful expression.

Gazing through the eyes of the vast cosmos, it feels as if we are on a journey of eternally becoming. The journey is one in which the soul is always growing. As a part of that growth, we incarnate to gain needed experience. Thus, the departure of the body, while significant, is not the ultimate end of the journey. It is a change. From this larger perspective, the departure of the body can be perceived as the ultimate *trompe l'oeil*, a painted artistic canvas that deceives our eyes. We visually perceive one thing, yet something altogether different is happening.

In death passage, a body that was once filled with vigor and purpose wanes day-by-day, filling us with despair. Yet, our core essence, the soul or eternal self, is strengthening and going unnoticed because we have not developed the conscious awareness to recognize this aspect.

> **Metatron:**
> *Death passage is dynamic, intriguing, and purposeful. Death passage calls forth a myriad of adventures that enliven the soul crossing. The consciousness is riveted towards precise action, which requires both profound awareness and enormous depth of purpose. Leaving temporary toys behind, the soul remembers the richness of the tapestry of Eternal Life.*

Soul Passage Midwifery seems to mirror the experience of death passage through engaging in a process of releasing, deepening, and expanding. Like walking a labyrinth, our awareness moves deeply inward and then expands outward. On the inward journey we are releasing preconceived notions and judgments about who we are, why we are here, and where we are going. We are moving into the core of our hearts to peer through a window that we thought was locked shut but which opens readily to an amazing world. On the outward journey we alter our perceptions of reality through expanding to meet other worlds and welcome them into our own. Like Lucy in C.S. Lewis's *The Lion, the Witch and the Wardrobe*, we enter what seems to be a closet in which we could become trapped but actually opens to stunning experiences:

> "This must be a simply enormous wardrobe!" thought Lucy, going still further in and pushing the soft folds of the coats aside to make room for her. Then she noticed that there was something crunching under her feet. "I wonder is that more moth-balls?" she thought, stooping down to feel it with her hand. But instead of feeling the hard, smooth wood of the floor of the wardrobe, she felt something soft and powdery and extremely cold. "This is very strange," she said, and went on a step or two farther.
>
> Next moment she found out what was rubbing against her face and hands was no longer soft fur but something hard and rough and even prickly. "Why it is just like branches of trees!" exclaimed Lucy. And then she saw that there was a light ahead of her—not a few inches away where the back of the wardrobe ought to have been but a long way off. Something cold and soft was falling on her. A moment later she found that she was standing in the middle of a wood at night-time with snow under her feet and snowflakes falling through the air.
>
> Lucy felt a little frightened, but she felt very inquisitive and excited as well.

In my experience, the changes of awareness through which one travels in death passage often happen instantaneously. One sees and is experiencing one world in one moment and suddenly, sees and is experiencing an altogether different world the next moment. Like

Lucy, one may feel a little frightened but also inquisitive and excited. When each of us truly understands that we are not these bodies, the reality of the soul emerges. We become one with the higher vibration of the next realm.

Consciousness is propelled through deliberately placing the attention in the correct manner, which means focusing on a frequency that is at a higher level. Thus, the pages that follow offer different perspectives on which to focus the attention throughout a death passage in order to hold the self at a higher level. Each perspective has its own story that does not necessarily seem logical to the mind. Like overlapping petals of a flower, these various perspectives somehow fit together with other people's perspectives to form a much larger whole. As awareness of the Great Beyond broadens, we feel the interwoven dimensions, the loving assistance from the Higher Realms and the profound reality of our true soul essence. Fears of death quickly melt in the presence of such a vast truth. What was once regarded as the greatest moment of tragedy becomes the key to entering Radiant Beauty as the poet Nancy Wood expresses:

> *In this hallowed place, life begins anew.*
> *In this hallowed place, I am the continuous breath*
> *of all that has gone before*
> *and all that follows after.*

And now here is my secret, a very simple secret. It is only with the heart that one can see rightly; what is essential is invisible to the eye.

Antoine Saint Exupery (*The Little Prince*)

Chapter Four
Releasing, Deepening, Expanding

Death Passage Midwifery is an incomparable journey into the depths of the universe. Imagination is sparked in ways that reminds me of early childhood. There is so much to learn that curiosity leaps with confidence into the joyful exploration. Through a continuous process of releasing, deepening, and expanding, each of us can fully participate in this wondrous adventure.

This does not mean that the complexities of the body disappear. Rather, it means that once one sees from a greater perspective, there is purpose to each step. With outmoded belief systems, it is as if one is locked into a swollen thumb after hitting it with a hammer. From this perspective, one can only feel the chaos and severe pain. Once we remember the larger awareness—the full body awareness—then we can apply ice and know for certain that the thumb will heal. Similarly, from the limited perspective of physical awareness at the time of death passage, all we can see is the body struggling. Once we see from the larger perspective of spiritual awareness, the beauty cast from the Radiant Light helps us to see that all is well, and that the soul births with cosmic splendor. From this larger perspective, those left on earth do not walk away empty handed. Rather, they walk away with expanded awareness regarding the journey of the soul.

Releasing does not happen in a vacuum. Light Beings are available at all times to assist such efforts. These beings respond to all requests for assistance at the time of a death passage or soul birth. They are not bound by any religion so all people may call on them freely. Throughout this chapter, Archangel Gabrielle, Archangel Jophiel, Butterfly Maiden, White Eagle, Metatron, Archangel Sandalphon, Archangel Raziel, and Archangel Azreal share insights to help efforts in releasing limiting beliefs. Additionally, one can call upon one's soul, who can see from the larger perspective. In this chapter, my soul shares her perspective regarding death passage or soul birth.

Thus, releasing outmoded beliefs and understandings ultimately reveals the beauty lying just beneath the surface, which is entirely accessible. While it feels like we are learning something new, when one experiences the expansion, one wonders how one could have forgotten.

Releasing

Releasing Preconceived Ideas and Beliefs
If we wish to be fully present with someone who is crossing the threshold, we must release all preconceived ideas and cultural biases about who we are, what a death passage is, and where we are going. What this means is, like the person going through the death passage process, we need to look at the process with different eyes. This

cannot be overemphasized. What we have been taught to navigate this earthly plane of existence is largely irrelevant in the Greater World. Through letting go, one is committing to take a different path. In taking this different path, one opens to receiving new information moment by moment.

To have a different experience, we must enter the higher realms deliberately through placing the attention with a word or feeling that bears a correct vibration. Entering with curiosity is a correct place of entry. Entering with a yearning to understand a different reality is a correct entry point. Otherwise, it is like wanting to swim in the ocean by going shopping in New York City. It is not a correct entry point. Professing to take a new path through going shopping brings considerable frustration.

Similarly, if we wish to change our experience of death passage, we must practice with tools, which are relevant to the expanded realms. We become students, expanding awareness step by step. At first, what is germane seems unusual. Guideposts for accomplishment are different. Once practiced; however, the new path invites ever-new awareness, which excites depth of knowing. We ultimately bound forward absolutely certain it is the correct path.

Butterfly Maiden:
If one wishes to fly, one cannot bring the cocoon and one cannot stay locked inside.

The words of Butterfly Maiden encourage us to make change so that we might fly. This means that if we release outmoded belief systems, we have every opportunity to experience something larger, which is very precious. Staying locked in the cocoon promises to bring the same difficulties that have always been.

Releasing Habitual Patterns

Releasing is a process of letting go of our habitual patterns surrounding death. We are setting them aside, perhaps placing them on a shelf where they can be retrieved if necessary. We are committing ourselves to learning a different way of understanding the death passage process. We are stepping into a new arena where anything is possible. This is not a scary place. It is a place of intrigue, of curiosity, of yearning to experience something more than what has previously been. Soaring beyond requires letting go to grab hold of something far greater. Changing the operating belief is like a rock climber securing the ropes at a higher elevation to ensure scaling success. Such an athlete does not dupe the self into believing that he or she can scale the cliffs without the assistance of the ropes. The ropes not only provide safety but also allow athletes to climb higher and more adeptly than previously imagined. Likewise, for a soul passage, securing the path forward requires releasing old patterns to grab hold of the more expanded awareness to secure the path forward.

> **Soul Perspective:**
> *I stand beyond the place where the stitches were formed.*

My soul assures me that her perspective allows the comings and goings of life to proceed unencumbered. Mistakes may be made on the physical plane but one does not have to enter into any tug of war that may ensue. One expands one's awareness to stand beyond the place where such a reaction might feel warranted. From this expanded awareness, only a loving response comes forth.

Recognizing that one needs to change the path, one commits to a new practice that leads to a new path and a new experience. In essence, we are releasing entering the experience through the eyes of the judgmental mind, and are instead entering through the eyes of the wise heart. A simple practice, which supports this new perspective, is a three-step process.

1. Shift the attention from the mind perspective to noticing the breath going in and out. Simply notice and observe for a few minutes.
2. Gently take deeper breaths and longer spaces, thus slowing the breathing rate.
3. Bring the attention to deliberately focus on the heart. Begin breathing deeply and slowly into the heart.

Breathing into the heart shifts the attention from the habituated judgmental mind to the gentleness and brilliance of the heart, which is an expression of the soul or core essence. This practice alone changes lives daily. Instead of noticing all the things that are wrong and judging them, one now notices all of the things that are right and embraces them. This awareness continuously naturally expands, resulting, over time, in conscious awareness of higher realms. From the spaciousness of the heart awareness, one can then inquire of the soul perspective. When I asked my soul about death, I received the following:

> **Soul Perspective:**
> *Impulse. Expansion. Impulse. Expansion.*
> *All growth is continuous. All life is continuous.*
> *What is no longer needed falls away. The new is in place before that occurs.*
>
> *When one is faced with a death passage or soul birth, a new node has been formed from an impulse and then it is time for the expansion. The process of life has been building the new node, and when it is complete, the expansion occurs naturally.*

Energetically, all of life is continuous. A death passage is a new birth. The energy continues. Thus, my soul is telling us that life goes on. The soul or core essence is the energy, which is continuous.

The expansion occurs naturally. The new life is already in place. I remember when my mother crossed. I passed her into the arms of the Christ before her body quit breathing. Thus, Spirit takes delicate care in the overlapping of dimensions to have everything in place before the body falls away. The emergence of the soul is a result of all that comes prior and it happens naturally.

Releasing Fear of Death

A part of the terror of death is the belief held by our culture that death passage is something negative. Life on earth is the supreme expression. There can be nothing more or better. People in our American culture simply do not wish to even talk about death or death passage. We seem to condemn aging as if it were a sickness. Ram Dass finds that our culture considers "aging a failure, that somehow God made a big mistake. If God were as smart as the commercials, people would be young forever." While religions teach that it is positive to enter into eternal life, there has not been adequate instruction in the Western world to meet this sacred task. In every other aspect of our lives we are given enormous information and preparation for our next step, whether it be obtaining a driving permit or applying for graduate school. Only in the arena of death passage are we met with a stony silence.

Engaging death passage as a part of the circle of life allows the natural flow of existence to flourish. Otherwise, we are meeting a natural process with our heels digging into the dirt. We are telling the baby not to come out of the womb. This stance actually complicates an otherwise natural phenomenon, which creates tension, exhaustion, difficult emotions, and unnecessary actions for the person departing and the family.

We all understand the genuine human sadness of saying good-bye. Our compassionate nature rises up for Gabrielle having to say good-bye to her children, for young lovers being separated, for a wife leaving a husband behind. Yet, for consciousness to energetically move unimpeded, we must deliberately focus our attention on the higher way. Feelings of anger, despair, and grief definitely impede the natural process because they color one's awareness. Therefore, practicing the heart breathing is of utmost importance to help keep one's perspective in the correct arena. Such a practice is extremely valuable when facing a death passage. This does not mean that one won't have work to do after the passage, but it does mean that one meets this sacred task holding vivid beauty as the call as Archangel Gabrielle explains.

Archangel Gabrielle:
The feelings of the human form are a beautiful expression meant to deepen experience. Likewise they give warning to resist moving in a direction that is not positive. When meeting feelings, which overwhelm, turn and face the sun. Walk towards the sun taking the warming into the heart while leaving the provocation behind. The heart processes anything, which is off center. It does so through transmutation. Use this wisely when a death passage is imminent.

Archangel Gabrielle invites us to use overwhelming emotions as a moment to reflect rather than to express. Take a walk. Face the sun and practice heart breathing to help transmute the strong emotions. Once the appropriate balance is achieved, the expanded awareness can return. This harmonious frequency is essential when assisting another to cross the threshold.

Archangel Jophiel:

Judgment is a very harsh assessment of any situation. People behave in similar ways in similar circumstances. Compassion for the difficulty is what is needed. Let all thoughts of harshness continue moving; do not embrace their expression.

Archangel Jophiel assures us that judgment is not our task. This position comes from the mind, not the heart. Compassion springs from the heart so work always to keep this perspective at the forefront.

"Let all thoughts of harshness continue moving." Just because a thought pops in the mind, it does not mean that we must embrace it. Archangel Jophiel is recommending that we allow a harsh thought to continue passing by.

Butterfly Maiden:

The cocoon becomes hardened when built of limiting beliefs and extreme emotions. Sweep emotions clear through self-reflection and purifying thoughts. Cast aside beliefs, which create separation.

Cocoons are ordinarily soft though secure like the embryonic sac. Yet, Butterfly Maiden explains that this protective shielding can become hard from limiting beliefs and extreme emotions. The flexibility required of it is lost. She thus recommends deep self-reflection. Instead of embracing the expression of a harsh emotion, act instead to purify that expression with a loving thought. This is a valuable practice at the time of a death passage.

Releasing the Being Crossing or those Staying

When participating in a loved one's passage, give verbal permission for the person crossing to go. This brings relief to those going and those staying. Souls preparing to cross the threshold consider everyone. If it is at all possible to say good-bye in person, they will wait. Those departing will also wait for others to be ready before taking the last breath. Georgiana waited for her daughter to arrive until finally the energies would wait no more. My father was hesitant to leave because he did not wish to cause me the pain, which he experienced at my mother's passing. Lisa did not wish to leave her children or husband, so she prolonged her life in the face of great pain even though she had no way to alter the course.

> **White Eagle:**
> *Distant drums speak to the heart whether holding one back or giving a fresh start. Give the true gift to all departing souls.*

White Eagle implores us to give the "true gift" to all departing souls. It is not for us to determine the correct rhythm of a soul's journey. Rather, it is for us to understand that each soul has his or her own path to follow. When we can give the "true gift," we help relieve the soul passing of an extra burden.

Butterfly Maiden:
Release others to release oneself.

This is an interesting quote. Butterfly Maiden shares that actually, in releasing others, we are indeed releasing ourselves of an unnecessary burden. This applies to those departing and those staying on earth.

Deepening

Embracing Stillness

After releasing limiting perspectives, we shift our attention to deepening. To deepen, we befriend stillness. My soul shares her expanded insight regarding deepening.

Soul Perspective:
Holding stillness as a pillar within is essential for Soul Passage Midwives.

It is from this point that one can perceive the more subtle realms. Opening to receiving information to assist, requires absolute clarity of intention, purity of heart, as well as stillness of mind and being.

When one is able to hold stillness there is no attachment to how the process proceeds. It unfolds creatively each time. There are no expectations. The conversations and events are always in the moment. Decisions as to course of action are instantaneous.

From the soul perspective, stillness is essential for deepening. This is not a haphazard approach. It is a very focused, attentive awareness of the soul. With this deliberate stance, the Soul Passage Midwife can meet each challenge as needed, from the larger perspective, in the correct manner.

Forgiving Others and the Self
To be appropriately available to assist someone across the threshold, we must forgive others and ourselves, for all negative encounters whether intended or unintended. This process alone releases one from emotional entanglement, which often takes the forefront of our attention in times of perceived crisis. The freedom gained from the release of these chains is blessed. From this practice, we begin to see events, as they are from a greater perspective rather that how we would like them to be or how we misperceive them to be from our limited vantage point. This practice helps us to release our attachment to our current perception of reality. We let go. We let go of all of our attitudes about others and understand that in the larger reality their actions are recorded. It is not for us to judge. It is for us to have compassion. Thus, we forgive. We ourselves are forgiven. Thus, we forgive.

One way to make the shift to the greater reality is to see a loved one as a soul on a journey, which has been fraught with perils. Sometimes this soul has triumphed and sometimes this soul has much more to learn in a given arena. We then become souls bearing witness or pilgrims on the journey rather than mothers or fathers, daughters or sons. If participating in a death passage, our job is to be present in every moment to help the soul making the journey. Nothing else has priority. While we have other things we must do, we are always holding the person crossing in the highest light and making decisions from that perspective.

>   **Soul Perspective:**
>   *Holding stillness carries one through difficulties. One must be still and unwavering at one's core, moving with precision and being unwilling to become misaligned for any reason. With this focus, there is no conflict, no challenge presented. One simply moves forward undaunted as the path is illuminated each step of the way.*

My soul again encourages stillness. Notice the words "unwilling to become misaligned for any reason." Alignment is critical. Paying attention to this alignment is of the highest order. Holding the correct frequency is a core ingredient that is not taken lightly. When holding the correct frequency, forgiveness is implicit. There is no conflict. Seeing from the higher awareness, love is the only response.

We also continuously forgive ourselves for any lacking or misperception. Understanding that we have done our best, we move on to embrace ourselves as a part of the Greater Plan. We bring our focus to bear on the situation from the Greater Perspective thus opening the gate for holding steadfast.

Appreciating All

While sitting with our loved ones we can think about all the things we appreciate about them and let them know. We appreciate the time with them, the colorful flowers that are blooming, the melodic music we hear, and the unwavering kindness of others helping us at this time. This approach helps us focus on the Greater Awareness and bring that loving energy into the sphere of the experience. This is not a false appreciation; often we notice things we have never noticed before. Thus, it is an excellent practice in seeing through different eyes.

> **Archangel Jophiel:**
> *Appreciation brings blooms to plants in the Spring, smiles to faces once torn and joy to hearts long in the desert. Look through different eyes to see hidden beauty joyfully present. This is the thread that can weave a new tapestry.*

Archangel Jophiel encourages us to use appreciation as a daily practice. If it can bring blooms to plants, smiles to faces once torn and joy to hearts in the desert, it can bring peace into our hearts at the time of a soul passage. This is the very thread that can help us each weave a new tapestry, bring in brilliant color, and start anew with a fresh perspective.

> **Archangel Gabrielle:**
> *Appreciation is the golden key to unlock doors thought permanently closed. Shifting to this awareness releases the*

cobwebs long accumulated. A marked ease comes into the life of one who sees through these eyes.

Archangel Gabrielle resonates and repeats the insight to work with appreciation. This can unlock doors thought permanently closed! This is a powerful perspective. Seeing through these eyes releases cobwebs and brings marked ease into one's life. Making the effort to see through these eyes can make change in one's daily life absolutely.

Embracing Oneness

Embracing Oneness helps us to feel the presence of the One energy flowing through all that exists. We have a shared origin, a shared path, and a shared destination. Formlessness is an ever-emerging essence, which permeates all and gives rise to all. Once we have tapped into this perspective, we begin to see through different eyes.

> **Soul Perspective:**
> *One must make way for the more subtle energies and allow them space in the midst of the tumult of a death passage. The starkness of the material world commands immediate attention, which most give out of habitual instinct. Only through choosing to relate to the world in a different way can one begin to unravel the Mystery.*
>
> *Divine Essence moves with gentle assurance through every challenge to create resolutions that astound. When one can*

> *allow space for this seemingly nonexistent energy, even the most intense bellowing in the material world will not stand.*

Notice that my soul is very explicit in stating that, "only through choosing to relate to the world in a different way, can one begin to unravel the Mystery." There is a choice required of us at the time of a death passage. We can actually stay immersed in the limiting patterns if we wish. The gift offered if we choose to take a more expanded path is for us to "begin to unravel the Mystery." This is a profound statement that assures us that moving in this direction absolutely correct.

> **Butterfly Maiden:**
> *Cast aside beliefs, which create separation.*

Butterfly Maiden states unequivocally that we are to cast aside any belief, which creates separation. This is fundamental. Working harmoniously with Spirit requires an underlying understanding of the concept of Oneness.

Understanding Oneness through exploring the terms positive and negative space can also assist deepening efforts. This way of perceiving the all-present energy is borrowing terms from the art world: positive and negative space. Positive space is that space which we all perceive as human beings: trees, buildings, or all the things that exist in this world. Negative space is all the space in between what we perceive exists. The space between is where the work of Divine Essence transpires, as Nancy Wood beautifully captures in her poem "Beads of Life":

> *The space between events is where*
> *most of life is lived. Those half-remembered moments*
> *of joy or sadness, fear or disappointment, are merely*
> *beads of life strung together*
> *to make one expanding necklace of experience.*
>
> *The space between events is where*
> *we grow old. From sunrise to sunset one day lives*
> *as another day emerges from the fluid womb of dawn,*
> *the first bead strung upon*
> *the everlasting thread of life.*
>
> *The space between events is where*
> *knowledge marries beauty. In quiet reflection*
> *we remember only the colored outline of events,*
> *the black and white of war, the rosiness*
> *that surrounded our first love.*
>
> *The space between events is why*
> *we go on living. The laughter of a child or*
> *the sigh of wind in a canyon becomes the music*
> *we hear expanding in our hearts each time*
> *we gather one more bead of life.*

Universal Love

Universal Love is different from the everyday definition of love. It is much more expansive, forgiving, aware, and generous. We open to Spirit entering into the equation by focusing on this higher Love.

> **Archangel Jophiel:**
> *Universal Love applies love only to all situations and forms.*
> *It is an eternally emerging pure essence that is the antidote*

for all difficult states of being. Shifting to this perspective is something the angels help humans experience. Once one has been immersed in this feeling, it is not forgotten.

Archangel Jophiel shares that Universal Love is an "eternally emerging pure essence." This tells us that it is not a static energy. It is rather very dynamic: emerging, then emerging again, ever renewing the space and the beings within that space. One can imagine this as a geyser ever renewing itself from within the Earth to climb ever higher in its expression

We can take heart in knowing that angels help humans to embrace the perspective of Universal Love. Thus, one must not become discouraged. For if angels are helping with this, then all people are prone to challenges when entering this vibration.

> **Archangel Gabrielle:**
> *This requires stepping out of the realm of personal. Universal Love exudes compassion for all beings in all circumstances. It is a calling forth of the understanding of the soul lesson, which allows one to move from this perspective. Holding care and compassion for a soul crossing the threshold helps one to step into Universal Love.*

Archangel Gabrielle counsels that an expression of Universal Love is compassion. By looking at a death passage as part journey of the soul and part lesson, one comes to compassion quite readily.

Expanding

Remaining Conscious

Taking the time to be conscious in our every effort allows expanding to naturally emerge. This is incredibly powerful. For the soul crossing the threshold, the new life unfolds. For the souls witnessing, a new way of seeing unfolds.

> **Archangel Gabrielle:**
> *Long remembered chains of sadness are broken, to be no more. Freedom is gained at a cost never too high. The lessons of a perceived cage become apparent for all to see. The Great Song carries the wind.*

Archangel Gabrielle counsels that the price for freedom is never too high because the soul learns so much through the journey on earth. The lessons of being in the body are worth what the soul gains in every way. The Great Song harmoniously continues to move forward as souls learn and grow.

Recognizing Pure Essence

> **Archangel Raziel:**
> *Dreams of Eternity were here all the while. The Great Torch lights the way. Seeing clearly, we are befuddled no more.*

Archangel Raziel shares that eternity is in our midst at all times. The Light is ever available and shines to guide the way. Once we recognize this pure essence, we move with an entirely different understanding.

For those witnessing a soul passage, the expanded interchange with the Absolute radically alters life. No longer does one acknowledge limitation. In every action, one begins to notice the expanded awareness and yearns for this to be the way of life. For those departing, moving into Radiant Beauty is a profoundly joyful moment.

Being Present in Both Worlds

Expansion is being present in the Expanded World as well as being here on earth. We can experience both worlds simultaneously at the time of a soul passage. In holding the highest vibration, we give every opportunity for seeing and understanding this passage anew as well as for the departing soul to have a gentle passing into Radiant Beauty.

Interestingly, this is actually a possibility in every day life. A glimpse at the time of a soul passage represents an opportunity to bring this awareness into our world here. Along with many other seekers, I have encountered this type of awareness in many earthly circumstances such as driving or teaching. This is the new way—palpably moving gently into our world moments at a time.

The Soul Passage Midwife or family member deliberately focuses his or her attention at the space beyond birth and death. One stands between worlds. This is a critical understanding. Conscious awareness can see in all directions. Imagining the self as a circular rainbow expanding beyond earth into the heavens helps move one into this awareness. From this perspective, one accesses the soul or core essence that moves from the awareness of all eternity.

Soul Perspective:
Soul Passage Midwives are adept at being in both worlds at once. They know how to pay attention to the Subtle Realms and the cues that guide the way. Soul Passage Midwives understand holding the correct vibration in the face of the great storm of death passage. Their vision is clear and they cannot be pulled into the tumult.

My soul tells us that holding the correct alignment of clarity is critical. Winds may toss and turn but the Soul Passage Midwife stands steadfast.

Arriving Home

Archangel Sandalphon:
The cosmos is seized by the atom. One soul contains the All. Home.

Archangel Sandalphon states that we are each a microcosm of the macrocosm. Everything contained in the Cosmos is contained in the soul. We are made of the essence of the All. Realizing this is the true Home.

Archangel Azreal:

The joy of my role realized. The trick of the Universe revealed. Welcoming is a beautiful task. The dreariness projected by humans who have forgotten; erased.

Archangel Azreal assures us of the great beauty involved in her role in the cosmos. She welcomes souls home from a challenging journey. Humans tend to think her task dismal. In actuality, humans have forgotten the beauty of the Expanded Realms. Once one participates in a conscious soul passage, one remembers the true reality and the dreariness is erased.

Archangel Jophiel:

From this perspective, one can see that death is actually a birth into the heavens. The Cosmic Celebration is felt in the heart relieving the person of unbearable grief.

Archangel Jophiel assures us that this approach is the way to experience a death as a birth into the heavens. As we have learned earlier, the joy felt in the heart greatly mitigates the unbearable grief. One recognizes the Cosmic Celebration and remembers his or her place in the Cosmic Symphony.

※

Gleaning Understanding:
Releasing, Deepening, and Expanding provide a process, which can become a part of one's every day life. It is a way to reflect and assess

where one is as a soul. Through practicing this awareness before a soul passage, one becomes fluid with the process. It then becomes a self-correcting ritual.

Insights for Those Preparing to Cross Over:
- Release preconceived ideas about what a soul passage is, and embrace what is about to transpire with curiosity.
- Try to see your personal life through a larger lens, thus embracing the higher awareness that life goes on in a different way.
- Notice experiences you have along the way. What are they trying to tell you about the upcoming journey?
- Work steadily to embrace and understand the soul perspective through heart breathing.

Insights for Families and Professionals:
- Release preconceived ideas about what a soul passage is, and embrace what is about to transpire with curiosity.
- Deliberately place your attention for the journey at hand. This is a cosmic birth, a soul birth, and an amazing celebration.
- Assist the person crossing in choosing to see through a different lens of perception.
- Make time to practice breathing into the heart daily. Assist the person crossing the threshold in practicing this technique.

Conclusion

Bringing the experience of death back into the circle of life opens doors that have long been closed. Releasing preconceived ideas and cultural biases about death passage reveal new paths for us to explore ourselves, through which we can come to our own conclusions. From this place of the knowing, we can make wise choices from the soul perspective.

My personal experience has been that this exploration brings Radiant Beauty palpably into our midst, which greatly mitigates the unbearable grief. Placing the attention deliberately is an important aspect of the journey. Angelic Beings from the Expanded Realms assure us that the passage into the Great Beyond is a celebration. Through placing our attention in the correct manner, we can perceive this birth and the soul's amazing welcome Home.

Breathing into the heart helps each of us to remember our own soul perspective or core essence, which connects us to the whole of the Cosmos. This stalwart being can, indeed, guide us through any and everything, including the conclusion of life on earth or birth into the Great Beyond.

Gone was the sorrow if parting. The pity and grief for his death, long the robber of my peace, now fled in stark shame. Bliss poured forth like a fountain through endless newly opened soul pores.

Parmahansa Yogananda, (*Autobiography of a Yogi*)

Chapter Five
Holding the Presence

I remember as a small child being told that we do not talk about death. My young mind was more perplexed about this than anything else. My thought was if everyone "dies," then surely it is a good topic for discussion. Still, going to heaven was about all that was said.

In my junior year in high school I was required to read *The American Way of Death*, an expose on the funeral industry. Like many young people in my class, I was horrified. That same year, my beloved dog and childhood companion died. I was stunned to silence that my dog was put to sleep without any warning or moment to say good-bye. Recovering from this experience was long and arduous.

When I was twenty-two years old, as a young woman, I was called to my paternal grandmother's bedside. My older brother and I spent some time alone with this amazing woman. We actually talked about her impending death. She was very clear. We asked if she was afraid; she said no. I carry this beautiful gift with me always. From this simple gesture, the healing of my heart was clear and life moved on.

PARMAHANSA YOGANANDA

When I read *Autobiography of a Yogi*, my heart ached as Sri Yogananda described the loss of his mother when he was only a boy, "When we reached our Calcutta home, it was only to confront the stunning mystery of death. I collapsed into an almost lifeless state. Years passed before any reconciliation entered my heart." The healing he sought finally came when the following words from Divine Mother entered his heart:

> *It is I who have watched over thee, life after life, in the tenderness of many mothers. See in My gaze the two black eyes, the lost beautiful eyes, thou seekest!*

This gives us insight into the heart of a great Master who wishes to share wisdom with us. Through lifting our vibration and expanding our awareness, we too can move through the grief to feel true peace.

Later in the book, Sri Yogananda inquires meticulously about life in the hereafter from his guru, Swami Sri Yukteswar. Sri Yukteswar vividly describes his new life in a chapter dedicated to his journey in the Great Beyond. The following excerpt gives a brief glimpse of the astral universe:

> *The astral universe, made of various subtle vibrations of color and light, is hundreds of times larger than the material cosmos. The entire physical creation hangs like a little solid basket under the huge luminous balloon of the astral sphere. Just as many physical suns and stars roam in space, so there are also countless astral solar and stellar systems. Their planets have*

> *astral suns and moons, more beautiful than the physical ones. Thee astral luminaries resemble the aurora borealis—the sunny astral aurora being more dazzling than the mild-rayed moon—aurora. The astral day and night are longer than those of earth.*

The detail and intrigue of this description give us information to take into our hearts to further our intuitive understanding of the Great Beyond. Imagine many different souls recounting their experiences for our collective benefit! From the simple examples given here it is apparent that more information inspires and heals our hearts. Rather than keeping death passage in the closet, it is imperative that we talk, share, and learn from our collective experiences.

Spirit can teach through any avenue, and indeed does so. Working through meditation is one such example. Instruction can be given as in a schoolroom using this technique. Once one has learned well how to listen, the channel is open new understandings.

Holding the Presence
On the 18th of June I enter my morning meditation and am met with the message that a devotee is preparing for her transition. I listen and watch the following:

> In my third eye, I watch myself drive to where she is. She and I then walk over to a special space for her to prepare. It becomes a "school" so I understand that this will be instructional for me. I help the devotee into the school and we find the room where she is to go. I assist her in walking down a ramp and we walk to a beautiful chamber where she will be. This vision changes to a

> Holy Temple, which is filled with many people and spiritual beings gathered to wish her well. I feel the enormous love and profound honoring that everyone holds for this unique soul. We walk up three steps and I help her into the elevated bedchamber where she is to lie down. When she is settled, it is time for me to depart.

Meditation practices always include deep focus through the third eye, which is located between the eyebrows. This type of practice is beyond the scope of this book since it resides at a much deeper level. For those who wish to pursue this work it would be a requirement to embark on a daily practice with a trusted, loving teacher and community.

As I enter my morning meditation on the 19th of June I am greeted with an addition to the experience:

> All of the beings gathered in the Holy Temple are chanting and singing with great reverence. My soul stands apart to observe and take instruction. Parmahansa Yogananda appears in his ochre robe looking as he does in the commemorative painting gracing the walls of his memorial temple in Ranchi, India. He hovers just above the devotee and those gathered sitting in the lotus position linking all together in meditation feeling the Holy Presence of the Infinite. This is called "Holding the Presence," I am told. I am shown that it is like nesting dolls with each unique frequency fitting just inside the one prior.

The value in holding a correct frequency is in helping the soul to align with this higher frequency step by step. As souls feel resonance with the higher frequency, the essence reorganizes through entrainment to express each higher level. Such a practice helps Light Beings and humans to work with the same process, which is incredibly powerful. Often humans are unknowingly working against such spiritual efforts during a death passage.

As I begin using this meditation in my work with assisting souls crossing, I can feel the steadiness of the frequency even as it changes to the next higher one. Through entrainment, souls readily adopt the correct frequency as it is presented. It is natural process and flow of energy. Also, it becomes obvious to me over time that many souls can go to the Holy Temple in the Higher Realms. This is totally beyond any one denomination. Both warm and welcoming, it feels like a point in consciousness where souls, angels, spiritual advisors, light beings from far and wide meet to work on issues having to do with spiritual realms; as in a familiar meeting place known throughout the Cosmos. I integrate this into my work and take souls to the Holy Temple if it is appropriate.

Reciprocal Frequencies

A further explanation of Holding the Presence is presented in this meditation on the 5th of July, 2010. Reciprocal Frequencies requires an energetic focus to help loved ones preparing for and moving through a transition.

Kindness......Joy........Precious Awareness.....The Great Song

Vortex pulling down

Don't get caught in the vortex

Thus, through Holding the Presence we are helping our loved ones with the antidote to the vortex of lower vibrational thinking. As we share kindness, joy, and precious awareness, we are a part of The Great Song moving with deliberate awareness through Love with nothing to obstruct. We are holding the correct frequency.

Parmahansa Yogananda has a special interest and often attends soul passages as remembered in Pricilla's passage:

> Pricilla is resting in the womb of the Great Mother, the muted stars as candles lighting the way, one brilliant throbbing star appears. In the Holy Temple, all beings are Holding the Presence, the correct vibration: Sri Yogananda, angelic presences, my soul, hushed, awaiting the birth.

Discussion

I would like to offer a further explanation of Holding the Presence. Simeon Nartoomid explains that the nesting theory is a foundational metaphysical concept in which vast energy becomes more and more individuated and then recalls and reabsorbs the individuated energies. This applies to the entire universe including moons, planets, stars, nebulae and smaller energies, such as human bodies, cells, protons, and neutrons. Being recalled through a death passage is a universal experience.

When thinking about Reciprocal Frequencies, research in the domain of sound healing offers a perspective for use in our every day world. In sound healing, it is a foundational application for wellness to use an opposite frequency to assist a person to reorganize at the cellular level. This has been demonstrated by the research of Sharry

Edwards. Thus, what works out in the universe also works here on earth for bodies. The more we can work in harmony with universal principles, the more smoothly life unfolds.

Prayer of Invitation

A Prayer of Invitation is an essential component to invite Spirit Beings to assist in Holding the Presence. This can be simple or more formal. My prayer for my mother was, "Please help her." They are the most important three words I have every uttered.

Prayer is an energetic technique, which sets up the connections between souls, between spirit and matter, and between worlds. This is not the last, but rather the first course of action. Use it always to set the correct tone and frequency for a soul passage.

INSTRUCTION FROM ANGELIC PRESENCES

Angelic Presences serve humanity. It is their deepest honor to assist in small ways and large. The only requirement is that they be invited. At the time of a death or soul passage, things need to be simple. Inviting the angels is a simple gesture that can bring beautiful awareness to a difficult situation. These beings are our best friends.

Angelic presences often appear to assist with soul passages. For Donald, there was an angel on one side and I was on the other helping his soul to walk small steps. For Andrew, there was a circle of angels holding the vibration while waiting for his knowing to return. Following the suicide of Dan, angels encircled both of us to help raise the vibration to a level where they could help him.

In March of 2011, while in meditation, I inquire whether there are Light Presences wishing to offer insights into death passage. The following Beautiful Beings shared brief instruction:

> **Archangel Jophiel:**
> *When making a transition, keep Radiant Beauty before you at all times by focusing on your heart center. Imagine all of the Angels of Light streaming into your heart each bringing a portion of the True Essence of Love to share with you. As you feel this enormous Love it automatically expands outward and you become present in a higher reality. When you find yourself there, believe it is true. All the Beings of Light are there to help you. When it is time for the transference of consciousness, focus on the being for whom you feel the greatest love. This being will assist you. If you prefer, you can continue to focus on Love as the Eternal Essence and the beauty inherent in this magnificence.*

This is a stunning quote to keep before you. Archangel Jophiel brings profound beauty with this instruction. She assures us that the angels are absolutely present to bring a "portion of the True Essence of Love," to share with each of us. This is not a lonely time; it is a time to be present with beings from the Higher Realms. Notice that as one feels this Love, it automatically expands outward. "Believe it is true," rings an absolutely imperative tone for resonance. Nothing can happen when one refuses to believe in the Higher Realms. Know that assistance is readily available when it is time to transfer your consciousness from the person to the soul. It is a beautiful moment.

> **Archangel Sandalphon:**
> *Reveal to thyself thy deepest prayer. Death passage is a journey inward navigating through the multitude of layers to the core of who you truly are revealing your deepest prayer. This is a beautiful process of unfolding and a blessed time to meet one's soul without all the trappings of earthly expectations and encumbrances. The purity of the True meeting cannot be demeaned in any way. When one goes forward in this Truth, the unveiling of the heavens is Radiance Ever Emerging.*

What is your deepest prayer? It is of the soul and the reason you came to earth. It takes effort to uncover something so pure. Making the effort is what Archangel Sandalphon is recommending. As you are moving through life and a death passage, this pearl beyond price reveals itself as the layers of misunderstanding are peeled away. This process "unfolds" naturally revealing the blessed time of remembering the soul or pure essence. Notice that Archangel Sandalphon assures us that the "purity of the True meeting cannot be demeaned in any way." He wishes for us to be totally clear on this point. Your soul is intact absolutely. Finally, we are to understand that we are an integral part of the constant motion of Radiance Ever Emerging.

Archangel Raziel:

Look to the dream state to instruct you in the ways of the heavens. Your consciousness is connected with all eternity and receives with gladness such messages. This is a very useful tool because the human mind is filled with misguided information so we must go directly to consciousness. All beings are able to be present in consciousness so are able to readily understand instruction given in this format. The appropriate level is automatically attuned.

We can understand the ways of the heavens through the dream state. Remember that I was sent many dreams of a black dress before my mother died. This aspect of consciousness is connected with the Cosmos. It moves and instructs in ways that are similar to what we experience in the Great Beyond. Instructions given in this manner can reach all beings because we are of the One. Also, the level of understanding is "automatically" correct for the person's level of awareness. Thus, do not believe that you are the only one who can't understand!

Archangel Gabrielle:

Gentleness through eternity comes with awareness. All beings crossing the veil begin to hear subtle talking for it is the nature of the higher realms. The magnificence inherent in the delicate fibers of subtle language brings Eternity to one's door. Listen for subtle tones to guide your way. Turn always towards the pulsing of gentleness. Harken only to the loving voice of peaceful ways as the eyes of a doe in the field or the song of the dove at sunset.

Archangel Gabrielle reminds us that gentleness is a hallmark of the ways of eternity. Telepathic communication is normal and natural in the Higher Realms. While this is subtle compared to earth communication, it is a true aspect of the Higher Realms. Listen for loving and gentle messages as you cross the threshold.

White Eagle:
Invite Wolf Spirit to carry the soul safely across the threshold. The Wolf Spirit holds the soul as a protectress so the soul can move swiftly within a quiet, loving container. Wolf Spirit goes directly to the Great Clan that calls. When the white feather appears in the sky, the Earth Clan knows that the soul has safely arrived in the Spirit World.

Indigenous people have always had a deep reverence for the things of Spirit and celebrate them in daily life. White Eagle shares this incredible knowledge that the feminine Spirit of Wolf serves as a 'protectress' for a soul to cross the threshold. We need never wonder of the generosity of the spirit of nature. Serving the One, this fierce yet gentle being creates a loving container to guide and carry the soul. She knows the destination of the soul by the Great Clan that calls. Notice the beautiful confirmation of the white feather appearing in the sky to let loved ones know of the safe arrival of the soul. Ancient practices were thoughtful of the soul crossing and those staying.

Butterfly Maiden:

Surround the soul with many layers of Love to melt away the encrusted difficulties of mundane life. Hold fast to the vision of complete transformation form chrysalis to butterfly flying free. This transformation of all souls releases anything holding them back be it belief, emotion or physical pain.

Butterfly Maiden brings the message of holding Love as the antidote to all of the difficulties of life. Envisioning complete transformation of the person to a great soul—from chrysalis to butterfly flying free—is a correct frequency and vision. Since it is of the higher order, this helps one passing with anything that may be holding one back whether it is belief, emotion, or physical pain.

Sush Al'Mundra (She Who Lights the World):

Walk with a Soul Passage Midwife who brings the soul to the Universal Bee Hive. The Great Mother infuses the Light within the Hive. The sound of the bees is the frequency that prepares the consciousness for the great change. Souls know to listen for this sound. The transference of consciousness takes place within the Universal Bee Hive.

These words are from an ancient feminine spirit who is now accessible to souls crossing the threshold. Maia Nartoomid tells us that Sush Al'Mundra walked the earth in ancient Turkey. Her return is another indicator that the Light of the Divine Feminine is pouring forth with uplifting frequencies. Notice that the sound of the bees, which is so loving and nurturing, is the indicator that one's time is at hand. Likewise, notice that the transference of consciousness from the person to the soul takes place within the protective shield of the Universal Bee Hive.

※

Gleaning Understanding:
Spirit Beings all work cooperatively. They go where they are needed and depart when the need has been fulfilled. It is such a beautiful symphony to experience. Holding the Presence is a simple, effective visualization and energetic focus from Sri Yogananda. The Prayer of Invitation invites Spirit Beings and Angels to participate in the crossing of the threshold. Once invited, these beings will assist in ways that astound, although often their efforts go unnoticed. Spirit Beings always answer at the time of a soul passage. Invite them by individual name, or invite them as a group.

Insights for Those Preparing to Cross Over:
- Take time to think about the Spirit Beings with whom you feel resonance. Ask now that they participate in your preparation.
- Make time to practice Holding the Presence. This is an important frequency that will help keep you steady in your crossing. Envision each change as a change in color like a rainbow.
- Select one or two angelic instructions with which you resonate to practice now.

Insights for Families and Professionals:
- Take time to practice Holding the Presence daily. As you do so, it will become a natural technique to use with someone crossing the threshold.
- Envision yourself expanding out into the Universe moving through different frequencies growing ever finer and changing color.
- Assist the soul crossing the threshold with holding the visions, which feel most meaningful to that person.
- Consider writing a Prayer of Invitation as a family to have ready.

Conclusion

The spiritual techniques given in this chapter are few and simple yet within the reach of all people helping someone across the threshold. Spirit stands ever ready to assist, so do not be shy. In every tradition, Feminine Spirits are becoming visible to assist at the time of a soul passage. There is much joy in the Universe as one takes this step of participating in assisting another's spiritual well-being.

In Tibetan the word for body is lü, which means "something you leave behind," like baggage. Each time we say "lü," it reminds us we are only travelers, taking temporary refuge in this life and in this body.

Soygal Rinpoche (*The Tibetan Book of Living and Dying*)

Chapter Six
Meditative Focus

Stilling the mind is an essential part of becoming a Soul Passage Midwife. This aspect of the self thinks it has the answers and asserts its opinions at every turn. Thus, one must be skilled in quieting the disturbance. One approach to working with this aspect is to create a single-pointed focus and hold the mind there. When the mind wanders, simply return it to the stated focus. With practice, the mind begins to focus more clearly and wander less. Thinking of the self as multifaceted and multidimensional also helps this effort. One is then simply holding a single aspect of the self, rather than the whole of the self, accountable for its focus and setting clear boundaries. This is a soul directive to which the mind responds.

In seeking to describe the state in which I am immersed when walking souls to the Other Side, I share five quotes from my journals. These five states of being can be used as meditative focus for Soul Passage Midwives and families planning to accompany loved ones across the threshold. Together they create a path through consciousness, which can be walked again and again.

I LOOK WITH WONDER, AWE AND REVERENCE TO THE SUSTAINING PRESENCE OF MY LIFE AND ALL LIFE.

It is from the above perspective that one enters the portal way into the Expanded World to witness the incredible beauty of a death passage or birth of new consciousness. Anything less does not contain the key.

When my mother crossed over, before I could be in this place I had to sob and sob. The overwhelming grief had to release before I could be in a place to receive the messages from Divine Essence. I returned to her room to find it filled with the majestic radiance of angelic presence and vivid color emanating from the subtle realms. It was like walking into an enchanted fairy kingdom with all the love, joy and deep peace that one would wish. My mother never looked more beautiful or pure. The flowers sang gently of the newness of life. Angels gave promise of caring for all of the details for which I had no answers.

In preparing for a death passage, we must look through this lens of perception. We cannot go forward dragging all of the perceived problems, which our minds have replayed and magnified over time. These problems do not have to be solved before we are allowed to transform. We need to grieve our monumental loss and deliberately shift the attention the higher awareness. When we peer through the eyes of the soul, we find a fluidity with this process that is welcoming.

I REST IN CERTAINTY THAT WE ARE ALL A PART OF ONE LUMINOUS ESSENCE PULSING IN THE UNIVERSE AT LARGE.

This certainty is a depth of knowing that does not waver. As a state of pure awareness, it is impenetrable by thoughts and emotions. The rhythm of Divine Heart beats always with clarity and purpose.

While I was singing to my mother during her last two hours here, all of the activities of the nursing home were in full blossom. She had been there for three weeks having been taken from the hospital to see my father who was upstairs recuperating from a massive stroke. There were carts moving up and down the hall, voices over the loud speaker, people coming and going. Outside there was a storm raging with all the intensity of a Hollywood production. None of this interfered. There was a purposeful rhythm to all, the dance of life on its various levels of consciousness playing out in my field of awareness: people helping people, flowers pulsing joyous color, lightning and thunder piercing the day, blessed angels helping my mother. While I had no idea what was going to happen next, I was absolutely resting in the Heart of Divine Presence.

We are one with Divine Timing and the Greater Rhythm. The shift to knowing that all is cared for is different from being immersed in the state of duality in which the mind reins. Knowing is a peaceful presence that acts more like a witness to the energy moving through its sphere of awareness. Things might be problematic but when released from judgment they are not empowered and thus fade. In spite of how things seem we must keep our thoughts focused on this higher knowing.

I LISTEN FOR THE NEXT INSIGHT TO BE REVEALED IN PURITY AND ELEGANCE.

This is definitely a receptive state where we always keep the door open for Spirit to show us the true way. Answers provided by Spirit are sublimely elegant in the most precise definition of the word. There is optimal use of energy and all needs are considered. Listening in this way removes the stress of having to figure out things beyond our sphere of accomplishment.

When I was walking my mother to the Other Side, I had no idea what might transpire next. In gazing intently through my third eye, I could vividly see that we were walking in a heavy fog. I didn't know what the fog was or where we were going. The only map was my internal sonar. So, I kept walking with my mom in my arms and I kept listening for the next insight to learn what to do. Meanwhile, on this dimension I was singing continuously at her bedside. I was absolutely focused and absolutely open.

When experiencing a death passage it is imperative that we become absolutely focused and stay absolutely open. We don't know exactly what is going to happen or how. What an amazing mystery! What if we listened for that next insight to be revealed instead of fearing what the culture wants us believe is catastrophe. How would this impact our journey? Certainly it is more joyful and creates many more options.

WHILE FIRMLY ROOTED IN THIS MOMENT, I ENJOY SURPRISES WHICH UNFOLD THROUGH THE CREATIVE PROCESS.

Nothing else matters except for this moment and this process. The curiosity aroused has us poised for action when the need arises. As a choreographer I work with improvisation to allow for the unfolding of the Mystery. No one knows exactly what will happen next or how the piece will develop. A movement challenge presents itself and an answer unfolds within the context of the current moment. Everyone celebrates enormously when a new expression emerges. The creation is genuinely embraced as a pinnacle of achievement felt in every heart.

As I continued walking in the fog with my mother in my arms, listening with the attitude of wonder, awe and reverence; resting in certainty that we are all a part of one Luminous Essence; firmly rooted in the moment, we came to a magnificent bridge. What a surprise this was! We had no idea where the bridge went, to whom it might belong, or what its purpose in the middle of the fog might be. In the spirit of the moment, we began walking over it. As we entered the Sacred Silence, we responded to this depth through becoming one with the silence. Angelic music then emerged moving us more and more deeply into sacred awareness. Staying receptive moment by moment while continuously deepening allowed us to take in the vastness of the love of the Christ.

With every soul's journey, the feeling emerges anew that there is incredible purpose in every moment and the ability to embrace this allows the space for creative unfolding to appear. The foregoing examples demonstrate this basic tenet: the Creatrix enjoys endless creativity. When we can be present in the moment, we celebrate this aspect of ourselves.

> **THE MIND DELIGHTS AT NOT KNOWING ALL OF THE ANSWERS. IT CAN REST IN FULL AWARENESS THAT IT WILL BE CALLED UPON WHEN NEEDED IN ITS AREAS OF EXPERTISE.**

In our challenge to move out of the constricted reality of the mind, entering through a higher portal way allows the mind to step aside without grasping to maintain control. When we learn to look with wonder, awe and reverence, stay rooted in the moment, rest in certainty that we are all a part of One Luminous Essence, and allow creative unfolding, we are open for attunement with Divine Essence. This is the very essence that creates universes with extraordinarily loving thoughtfulness for each delicate flower and each unique snowflake. Something vibrantly new can now emerge. Once this energy is fully embraced, the mind does not have to worry about having all the answers. In fact, in this state of consciousness it feels like the mind is happily in its proper place.

I did not question the voice or the experiences while in process with my mother, and yet, my mind did question intensely the next day, wondering if I had made it all up to help myself feel better. While I was in my parents' bedroom packing some things to take to the funeral home, I kept feeling like I had to lie down. At such a busy time, my mind thought that I had no room for idleness. Finally, the energies so intensified that I succumbed. As I allowed myself to relax, my mother appeared! She looked radiantly beautiful and had returned to say thank you! In the following months, she returned several times to bring me gifts from the Other Side. The first gift was a capstone of a pyramid, which she placed sacredly in my cupped hands. Truly, there are no words to express the feelings at having this connection.

※

Gleaning Understanding:
Meditation is an essential component to a soul passage. This is a way of listening at a critical time in life. The meditation can be a sitting or it can be walking a labyrinth or walking in nature. The uplifting frequencies are essential to the task at hand. Keeping this at the forefront allows higher frequencies to enter at will because the door is open.

Focusing the mind is an essential aspect of crossing the threshold. It does not have the answers for this situation and requires direction.

Insights for Those Preparing to Cross Over:
- Find a meditation practice to keep your mind busy in a positive way. Use the focuses given in this chapter or write your own.
- Observe your mind to try to understand how it works.
- Practice listening in meditation daily. You will grow in amazing ways.
- Try a walking meditation if you are able. Walk in nature. Walk the labyrinth.
- If you are not able to walk, bring nature into your space with living plants. Use a finger labyrinth sitting inside.

Insights for Families and Professionals:
- Practice meditation daily. Assist the person crossing the threshold to do the same.
- Find a labyrinth in your area. Consider taking the family to do this walking meditation together. When at the center of the labyrinth, offer a heartfelt prayer for a graceful transition for the loved one as a gift from all of the family.
- Help the loved one to create a finger labyrinth.
- Take time for the family to walk all together in nature. Quietly breathe in the healing frequencies and the inspiration.
- Learn to recognize when the mind is causing discomfort. Release it from its over working by bringing in expansive frequencies. Use the focuses in this chapter or write your own.

Conclusion

Participating in a soul passage can feel a bit precarious. One way through the rather daunting opportunity is to focus on the higher portal way and the new life while taking care of the daily tasks. When we do this, the mind relaxes, bringing ease into our lives in unexpected ways. Certainly this is consistently what I experience when walking individual souls to the Other Side. Divine Grace is ever present and ever flows into situations with the utmost caring and love. We are forgiven for all misinterpretations and ignorant actions. As we make way for the new life to be revealed through attunement with Divine Essence, we help open the path for a new way of perceiving death passage to become the norm.

One radiant energy pervades and gives rise to all life. While it may speak to us through plants, nature spirits or the human being, with whom we share life on this planet, all are reflections of the deeper reality behind and within them.

The Findhorn Community (The Findhorn Garden)

Chapter Seven
Death Passage as Creative Process

In Western societies we learn from a very early age that spirits cannot be visible nor are they real. Having grown up with such a mindset, we can often doubt the validity of the Unseen Forces even at the time of death passage. Soygal Rinpoche states that recognition is one of the greatest challenges in death passage. The Higher Realms are very subtle. The frequencies are different and we must adjust to them before we can see. Since most of us have not practiced this awareness in any consistent manner, we are left to coming to terms with it at the time of death.

Mystical encounters, dreams and visions are all a part of Soul Passage Midwifery and the creative process of dying. When we can listen to these messages instead of pushing them away, they inform us, prepare us, assist us, and love us. Grief, while definitely at hand, is not the only feeling present. A larger picture helps the energy to move. The unbearable loneliness that accompanies grief is greatly mitigated. We are not a fractured part of existence; we are in the midst of life unfolding. We are actively engaging the Mystery.

I was in my early forties when my parents crossed over. While obviously by that age people and pets had passed on, I had never been present for an actual crossing. When thrust into the midst of my mom's transition, I found my previous training and experience with creative process and dance improvisation to be most helpful in meeting the death passage with presence. Expanding consciousness as a container for such circumstances is something that can be learned by all. Creative process can be understood and practiced in an everyday setting. There are pointers to the correct path that can help individuals and families. While creative process alone does not replace the incredible value of meditation practice, it can open the door to stepping on the path of change in awareness.

Mystical encounters can be of great value at the time of a death transition. I had many such encounters over the course of the year preceding my mother's passage, One example occurred on Christmas Eve in 1992. I was meditating when Mary Magdalene appeared. Her message was "Look to the Universal Mother." I was of course astounded and deeply touched. At the time it did not occur to me that it was such a personal message. I assumed that it was meant for all beings to have this focus as the return of the Great Mother becomes a palpable presence in our world.

The second vision after midnight that evening was of the Christ. Again, I did not take the words spoken as a personal message. I simply thought he was reaffirming on his birthday that he is available to all of us. His message was: "Ye who are heavily laden, take my yoke." I encouraged myself to be more aware of working with Spirit with any challenges, which might be forthcoming.

Archangel Raziel reminded us earlier in the book to "Look to your dreams to instruct you in the ways of the heavens." In January of 1993 I began having recurring dreams about a black dress. These dreams continued until my mother called me to say that she had terminal cancer. Up until receiving her call, I didn't know what they meant.

From just these few examples, one can see that I was being prepared for the impending change. Can you understand how very thoughtful Spirit is in the face of important events looming? Putting the spiritual encounters together, they become a creative work in progress.

I feel mystical encounters, dreams, and visions are gifts from Spirit. There is no value in dismissing them as nothing; yet, we as a culture are prone to do exactly that. Following the crossing of the threshold of my mother, she appeared as a spirit form. In accepting her words as a gift meant for me, my heart soared and my concerns vanished. I knew my mother was beautifully situated. This is a creative process, an improvisation, an adventure into the Mystery, and a way to birth something new out of the situation. When engaging Vastness, the potential for the unusual is magnified intensely.

CREATIVE PROCESS

Listening, Allowing, Unfolding

Through creative process, one is listening attentively. One is allowing the energy to inform the process. The experience is unfolding moment by moment. This spaciousness brings an opening into one's awareness. Something new is being created. We enter into an interaction, an improvisation through energetic movement, music, vision, sound, light, conversation. While we might question the value of these unusual interactions with the Unseen, as we move past doubt and receive the infusion of greater energy, the feeling of celebration is unmistakable. This knowing then becomes a genuine part of our operating energetic. It is not a place of doing, it is a place of being.

Creativity moves where words do not, intuition serves as the guide. People engaged in producing a creative work are not bound by laborious analysis, their hearts take the lead. Soul Passage Midwives spend ninety percent of their time with listening, allowing and unfolding to create a unique path for each soul. This is a process of deep listening to allow the wisdom to reveal itself moment by moment. It's accomplished by conscious awareness that cannot be rushed. One cannot hold on to it, insist or demand. One allows it to unfold and gently emerge. It acts of its own accord, on its own rhythm, bearing its own message. Every facet of the experience is extremely interesting and intriguing.

Families are in a unique position to have extended time interacting with Mystery as their loved ones are preparing to make the transition. This time in life is one of intense focus and unusual circumstance. Thus, it is an important time to explore and rework beliefs and perceptions. While there is lots of activity that can take the entire focus, deliberately choosing to move towards conscious awareness opens doors not previously explored. The Mystery is actively working with loved ones and these energies are often visibly present. Worlds that were not previously apparent open to embrace us. If receptive, revelations emerge to greet us. Departing loved ones are often the guides because their frequency is expanding day by day. When we can meet them moment by moment using creative process, the energy can open us to new perspectives.

Listening is a key when elders' are preparing for a soul passage. They are going through many changes and will readily share these experiences if we are receptive. They are living moment to moment so we must meet them there. Three weeks prior to my dad's crossing he awakened to find the words "Thank you for all the wonderful care." Two weeks prior to my dad's crossing he called me into his room in the middle of the night and said "I can't live with you anymore." I inquired about where he might be going to which he replied, "To live with God." I found this amazing and tremendously comforting. Dad was ready and he wanted me to get ready. Had I not been receptive and listening I would have missed this vital information.

Spaciousness
Spaciousness is something that is felt viscerally with this approach. One is changing from a limited stance to an ever widening,

unlimited, indefinable and vast awareness. This expanding consciousness is not only of the body but also everywhere around the body. It can be as large as a room, a house, a country, a state, a nation, a continent, the Earth or beyond.

This spaciousness is something that I find difficult to experience in our Western society. Americans seem to be content to be confined to frantic schedules day and night. Such busyness negates the ability to notice and feel the beauty inherent in spaciousness. While there are times when we each must answer the call for an intense schedule, there is a need also to create moments for spaciousness in life.

Improvisation

Improvisation opens spontaneously once you engage in the creative process and experience spaciousness. This technique spans this world and the next. There is an interchange between listening and speaking, moving and stillness, song and silence, temporal and eternal. Deliberately placing the attention on such a technique invites this process to invigorate the energy.

Ultimately, creating something new out of what is no longer viable is the outcome. Thus, the body falls away because it can no longer function and the soul emerges into the next realm. This elegant design allows for life to exist temporarily on the earth plane.

DANCE BETWEEN WORLDS

In reviewing death passages chronicled earlier in the book, it is easy to see that each passage is unique. Each journey moves through creative process opening to spaciousness and improvisation. When working with souls, the Soul Passage Midwife meets souls as they are and proceeds from there. For example, when I first met Violet, she was encased in an energetic egg shape. Andrew was running in the desert towards distant mountains. Toby was in her hospital room. Townsend was expanding up and beyond his body to the ceiling of his room.

For Violet, the egg shape had to be dissolved before she could move forward. Andrew was already on the Other Side, having died suddenly, so I had to work on helping him understand where he was and encourage the return of the knowing. Toby's burning question, "What will it be like?" had to be answered before she could move forward. Townsend had no belief system, which allowed for anyone to expand beyond a body, ever. He could, however, see me, which was a huge help in calming him and beginning to forge an appropriate path.

Looking at this unfolding process from the creative perspective reveals a constant dance of energy. There are telepathic conversations, changing visions, and remarkable songs/sounds. Everything happens in the now. Soul Passage Midwives answer questions, dissolve fears, gently inform, and help ease the way. There are decisions that only the soul crossing over can make. One can think of the entire interchange as dramatic improvisation, musical improvisation, or improvisational dance.

Crossing the threshold involves interchanges between different beings including: Soul to Soul, Angelic Realms to Soul, Creatrix to Soul, Spirit to Person, and Returning Souls to Person. Each being moves in relation to the other. Each can be the initiator. Each can be a responder. Although the ultimate destination may be to become one with the All, there are many experiences at different frequencies between here and there, which can be explored for eternity if we wish. The following sections describe how the creative process and improvisations unfolded in each unique situation.

Soul to Soul

These are interactions between a person's soul to another soul who is either in the form of a person or in spirit form. All of the examples in Chapters 1 and 2 are written because of my soul's interaction with other souls.

Violet

I am most often called when people are having difficulty transitioning. For example, Violet was not getting better or leaving this dimension. After working with the challenge of the egg shape mentioned above, Violet had to come to a decision about staying on earth or moving to the next realm. We talked about the fact that she could choose either. Once Violet decided that she was going to cross over, an incredible decision on her part was to choose to go through what she called the nine hells. Never have I been so surprised for I know nothing of nine hells. Yet, my soul, very calmly stated, "That is not required of you." Anything could have happened at this point. Violet remained steadfast and replied, "I know, but I am going to go anyway." Then my soul had an improvisational decision to make. She told Violet that she should not go alone so she would go with her.

Andrew

Andrew was definitely in shock. He was on earth one moment talking on the phone, and then on the Other Side the next moment. Helping him to come to terms with this took some time. I had to listen to his story fully before he would even begin to hear anything I might say. "It shouldn't be so difficult to get home," he informed me. We conversed easily while drinking tea of divine nectar to help his frequency adjust. Realizing that I was the being that his friend had spoken about just prior to his death was pivotal in his being able to comprehend where he was. Andrew could not see the angelic beings in the circle until the knowing returned. Once that occurred, Andrew was ready to go with them.

Toby

Once Toby understood that she was not going to be annihilated as the mind had insisted, she was so excited that everything transpired quickly. "You mean I am not going to die die? I am just going to go live somewhere else?" We ran together, laughed, and talked about the thrill of being free. We welcomed the ancestors when they silently arrived in iridescent bubbles. There is no preparation for how other beings might appear in the Higher Realms. Thus, one is ready for anything!

Townsend

Townsend was indeed terrified. He had totally forgotten that he even had a soul. When I arrived, I said, "I know you don't believe in anything, but I am asking you to believe in me. And, I am asking you to trust me." He could have said no. Fortunately, he responded positively and his passage unfolded from there. By the end of our time together, when his knowing returned and he could see in the Higher Realms, he declared to Archangel Azreal, "I will forever believe in you." What a profound transformation.

***

Angels and Masters to Soul

These examples emerge when the Spirit Form of an angel or master enters in to the scenario in some way. Their purpose is to try to ease the way of the soul crossing the threshold.

Lisa

When Lisa was preparing for her passage, every twist and turn was ultra challenging. At one point, a circle of angels created a beautiful golden pool of water for her soul. When Lisa was submerged in this pool of warmth, she was able, at long last, to relax. Also through this method, her being was infused with frequencies she needed to make a gentle transition. This was a loving gift at a difficult time.

Gabrielle

Gabrielle was having difficulty leaving her children and husband. Think of Kali appearing to Gabrielle to purify destructive thoughts. Archangel Jophiel worked tirelessly to help Gabrielle see beauty in all its dimensions and forms. Many angels formed a circle around Gabrielle in the Holy Temple to assist her in expanding her frequency to reach the knowing. Angels are very present with souls throughout the process of a death passage. The Christ appeared to assist her transference of consciousness to the soul.

Corrine

Corrine's journey was profound in every way. In her journey we discovered the continuum of frequencies from Gaia through the Higher Realms as Corrine greeted beings from the elemental kingdom with fairies, gnomes, elves, and the spirit of Gaia honoring her. Angels and Masters were "Holding the Presence" for Corrine. Quan Yin and Kali were there to help her embrace the new beginning. Butterfly Maiden assured her that it was a sacred birth. Finally, the Christ and Mary Magdalene welcomed Corrine together. This inspiration assures us that Masters and angels keep their promises.

Townsend

When Townsend was having a difficult time from the very beginning, Archangel Azreal appeared to support him each step of the way. She and I were on either side of him throughout his process helping his exhausted soul to walk little steps. What an incredible effort on her part.

***

Creatrix to Soul

These types of spontaneous interventions often occur as a surprise in an ongoing scenario. Things are moving at a fairly consistent rhythm. Then suddenly, one statement or movement from the Creatrix changes the entire direction of the experience. There is no Spirit Form associated with this sudden intervention.

Georgiana

I was walking with Georgiana up the numerous stairs when we came to landing or perch, which was a precipice between worlds. Deep fog swirled around us. In that moment I heard an all encompassing voice instructing me to, "Leave her there." There was no being associated with this voice—the phrase reverberated though the heavens. My first response was that I could not leave her there. That was met with silence. I then quickly realized from whence it came and bid farewell to Georgiana. The resulting astounding experience is recounted earlier in the book. Sometimes the improvisation leads us to follow directions that are given to us in the moment.

Pricilla

Pricilla had many angelic presences and masters assisting her walk. The angels and Sri Yogananda were visibly "Holding the Presence" in the Holy Temple of La'kina to assist her transitioning efforts. Over time, each contributed in a beautiful way. In the final days when Pricilla could not let go, Spirit quite suddenly created a golden bird to assist her. I still remember this little bird rubbing its tiny head on Pricilla's cheek. She connected with the deep love of her soul for this little bird and was able to pass.

Donald

Donald's exhaustion improved only in very small increments until very close to his completion. At the time of his arrival, gorgeous celebratory singing erupted. We could see hundreds of ancestors and angelic beings encircling us in the form of a tulip blossom emerging from the lotus flower. This explosion of sight and sound caused Donald to jump up and ecstatically give the angel and me an exuberant hug of thanks.

My Mother

Think of the agonizing despair I felt as I was sobbing in a small room by myself. Think of my prayer, "Please help her." Then remember the angelic beings, pulsing orchids, and brilliant Light in my mother's room when I returned. The Creatrix hears prayers from the heart.

***

Spirit to Person

Spirit knows no bounds when creatively engaging in the soul passage process. The two hundred foot lily situated over Pamela's bed that served as her transport to the next realm is a good example of this. Another example is the warning to me from the Christ, Swami Sri Yukesteswar and Sri Yogananda that "The time is at hand," regarding my father.

Pricilla

Pricilla's ancestral song reverberates:

> *Oh Pricilla, can you hear us calling you?*
> *Oh Pricilla, we await your song so true.*
> *Can you hear us?*
> *Can you focus on the Light?*
> *We're here for you to welcome you to gain your truest sight.*

Remember that first stanza? The full song goes on to give an amazing amount of instruction by the ancestral choir. It is given in song so it will go directly through consciousness to Pricilla. Spirit wants to bypass the analytical mind and strong will that are challenging Pricilla. The singing also infuses the correct frequency needed.

Donald

Likewise, Spirit sent ancestral choirs to share insights with Donald. An all male choir sounded first, followed by an all female choir, which sang:

> *Hear thy soul*
> *Whispering*
> *Hear him call your name*
> *Blessed be*
> *Song of Truth*
> *Soon you will be free.*

Donald, although exhausted, listened with deep interest and began to open to the Spirit Realm.

Young Man

The experience with two young lovers who were parted due to a sudden accident is unforgettable. Spirit enlisted hundreds of angels to stand and Hold the Presence at each juncture where the frequency changed to allow for a direct infusion of Divine Love into the body of the young man. Clearly the young man was needed to continue on earth without his current love. She passed on and he stayed on earth. While tragic from the eyes of a person, it is a miracle from the eyes of the soul.

Jerry

Jerry actively insisted that he believed in nothing. Suddenly, White Eagle emerged from the Spirit World playing his drum and singing a chant to assist Jerry in letting go. The chant was:

> *One with the heartbeat*
> *One with the purrr*
> *One with the breeze that blows through the hair*
> *One with the Great Song*

Jerry's beloved dog was the first to greet him in the Spirit World. Jerry needed someone very trustworthy to open his heart to remember the knowing. The incredible thoughtfulness of Spirit at delicate, difficult moments continues to astound me.

***

Returning Souls to Person and/or Humanity

Souls often return after a soul passage to say thank you, to share messages to loved ones or to give a message for humanity. This type of encounter happens quite frequently following a soul passage.

Listening for this type of communication is an important effort after a loved one passes.

Paul

Returning souls very much want to be heard. Remember Paul's message to his parents that his soul life goes on and that he will see his parents again? He wanted deeply to comfort his parents by letting them know that he was fine and that he felt no pain at the time of the accident.

Gini

Gini shared great encouragement in the last stanza of her poem:

> *Waste no time, tarry not at the helm*
> *Take charge to create the new Loving Realm*
> *A bouquet of experiences I carry with me*
> *My song I send to say I am free*

James

I didn't expect to ever hear from my brother James again, and yet, years later he returned to let me know that his soul life goes on. He was strong with brilliant light and was with his divine feminine compliment. After such a tragic story as his, this brings loving encouragement to see things from a greater perspective.

Michael

Finally, think of Michael who wishes deeply for us all to awaken from the illusory dream in order to embrace the Truth of eternal life:

I harken you my friends
This experience now, to lighten and bend
Your focus in a new direction for good
Embracing Diving Love where I once stood.
We shall sing and dance and laugh once more
Because there is naught such a thing as death's door.

※

Gleaning Understanding:

Death passage offers an amazing opportunity to rework mental perceptions and expand limited beliefs. In reflecting about death passage, the beautiful awareness that emerges is that we are much greater than we realize and have much to celebrate. Interestingly, all of the lessons in this regard apply to life on earth as well.

Once understood, creative process can be used skillfully when preparing for a soul transition. Although any leap into the void may feel intimidating, we have within us all the skills necessary to make great change. This is not nearly as difficult as one might suppose. In fact, there is a feeling of simplicity after it is accomplished for both the loved one and the family. It is when we do not understand how that it feels very complex. Change in conscious awareness is what we are seeking. Following the path of listening, allowing, unfolding, spaciousness, and improvisation gently opens the door of our heart's yearning.

Insights for Those Preparing to Cross Over:
- When preparing for crossing the threshold, practice working with anything creative that delights your soul such as art, poetry, dreams, movement in small ways, music, or journaling. The importance of the experience here is to reach an impasse so that you have to practice listening, allowing, and unfolding. You can be listening for a word or sound. You can be clarifying a precise color. Whatever you choose must have deep meaning to you.
- Practice connecting with beings from your new Home including: ancestors, angels, masters, saints, star brothers and sisters. Trust that you will know when they actually appear. This is not something that can be conjured.

Insights for Families and Professionals:
- Make certain that the person crossing the threshold has access to creative endeavors of interest. Even passive listening to music can inspire the soul.
- Encourage reading, music, silence rather than television and news.
- Families have a wonderful opportunity to make this time creative for the family and for the loved one crossing. It is a much more positive use of the time available, which ordinarily hangs heavy. This change in focusing the attention can be uplifting for everyone. Try creating a beautiful wall that expresses deep love from the family and brings joy to all hearts.

- Professionals must tend their own creative awareness knowing that it is an important component of the work. Guiding families and loved ones becomes an artistic canvas, which emerges with color moment by moment.

Conclusion

Embarking on the journey with a broad understanding of listening, allowing, and unfolding as parts of a creative journey establishes a direction, which is a fundamental part of our souls or core essence as well as of the Higher Realms. Deliberately placing the attention in this way is a correct entry point because it spans across worlds. The language is understood on both sides of the veil. Spaciousness enters the experience as a significant part of it because the energy is expanding and spaciousness in inherent in its makeup. Improvisation with sound, light, other souls, other spirit beings, and other worlds is a natural outcome of this practice. Birthing of the soul is the creation, which emerges brilliantly as life continues on the Other Side.

Native people describe death as "a change of worlds."

Rainbow Eagle, (From "The Universal Peace Shield of Truths" in *American Indian Peace Shield Teachings*)

Chapter Eight
Interdimensional Communication

Interdimensional communication is a natural outgrowth of expanded awareness. Understanding its necessity, its value and the process are important aspects of allowing its unfolding in one's life. Many beings in the Universe are gathered to assist a crossing of the threshold so you can expect to have interchanges with them. Loved ones have experiences as their frequency is changing, which they may try to share. Families may experience beings trying to communicate with them. Soul Passage Midwives are engaging this process as they connect with their own souls and the soul of the person making the passage, as well as working with beings from the Higher Realms. This is a beautiful gift at a sacred time.

Receptive and Expressive Language
Communicating requires both receptive and expressive language. This holds true in communicating with the Mystery. Receiving information from Divine Essence is the feminine portion of the relationship. It is our receptive nature that invites and nurtures the subtle energies of the two-way conversation. This aspect is meditative, listening, and open to hearing the message. Prayer, song, and speech represent the other part of the equation. This aspect is

expressive, defining, and the masculine portion of the relationship. We need both aspects to have a two-way communication with the Mystery.

This begs the question, why are we not fluent with this communication with Spirit?

The Sacred Feminine

In our Western World, we live in a patriarchal civilization so the receptive aspect feels more foreign and largely unnecessary. In his book, *A New Earth*, Tolle describes the destruction of the feminine principle as one of the most devastating events in the history of our world:

> The suppression of the feminine principle, especially over the last two thousand years has enabled the ego to gain absolute supremacy in the collective psyche....Nobody knows the exact figure because records were not kept, but it seems certain that during the three hundred year period between three and five million women were tortured and killed by the "Holy Inquisition," an institution founded by the Roman Catholic Church to suppress heresy. This surely ranks together with the Holocaust as one of the darkest chapters in human history. It was enough for a woman to show love for animals, walk alone in the fields or woods, or gather medicinal plants to be branded as a witch, then tortured and burned at the stake. The sacred feminine was declared demonic, and an entire dimension largely disappeared from human experience…

Dr. Lauren Artress concurs that "we lost our connection to the invisible world." This connection is important to the creative process as Artress continues, "We turned against the imagination, grew to mistrust symbols, and devalued creativity. Our sense of the whole was lost. Unity is conceptually and experientially beyond the grasp of human awareness until we unify reason and image."

To assist us in regaining an understanding of navigating these waters, Dr. Artress has brought forth the remembrance of the Labyrinth as a tool for deepening our awareness through connecting with the Unseen world and our own souls. This is an incredible resource for Soul Passage Midwives and families. The design is based on sacred geometry so it carries within it sacred frequencies to help uplift and expand conscious awareness. It also acts as an amplifier for communication between Spirit and human.

Though the dates are somewhat different, both the Mayan Calendar and Vedic scriptures discuss earth cycles of approximately 26,000 years. These ancient teachings agree that there are cosmological cycles of which we are a part. We are in the midst of charting the overlapping frequencies of the close of one cycle and the opening of another.

Change is afoot and today we have people like Jean Houston who are celebrating the return of the feminine and the emergence of the "possible human." In her workshops she states that "these are the times and we are the people" as she has witnessed people all over the world awakening. Barbara Marx Hubbard talks of the evolutionary leap we are all making together to bring women into full and equal partnership with men. She states that this leap is "nonlinear, exponential and connected through the innovative." Maia Nartoomid writes of creating the New Earth Star when making this evolutionary leap and transfiguration. She has brought the gift of documenting the Sacred Feminine throughout the history of our planet as she helps us reconnect with our feminine spirituality.

With the resurgence of the feminine principle, women all over the world are awakening to lost gifts. Men are becoming more sensitive. Most of us cannot conceive of what is coming because we are products of modern society. Yet, the yearning is unmistakably present. Change is all around us even if we can't put a name to it. Stripping bare the Sacred Feminine is a root cause of the rigidity with which we view death passage. The awakening undoubtedly includes understanding the miracle of the birth into the heavens as our new way of being with death passage.

I do not believe cultures honoring the Sacred Feminine are afraid of death passage. Indigenous people understand for they have not ever given up believing in the Living, Breathing Essence that is our birthright. We owe them a huge debt of gratitude for their tenacity through the many years through which they have been continuously persecuted. Without their tremendous courage, this awareness may have permanently left the human psyche. Likewise, mystical traditions include the Divine Feminine in their ceremonial worship. They, too, deserve our thanks. Reclaiming this awareness is easier because of their tenacity.

Communicating with the Mystery

Exploring communication with the Mystery is a creative journey that starts with realizing a need for change. One way to find out what we actually believe in our hearts is to practice seeing this Divine

Essence from different perspectives. This is very personal and is different for every soul on the planet. While the process of death passage itself often changes long standing beliefs, it is good to inquire before such time so to be in a place of clarity when assisting the soul crossing. Following are some thoughts to consider in working through altering perceptions of interacting with the Mystery.

Open Yourself to the Mystery

By opening ourselves to a conversation with the Mystery or the Infinite, we are saying, please infuse this situation with the wisdom of Vastness. We are asking the question *How?* The blank canvas is at our doorstep. We embrace creative process as our template for negotiating this path.

The following poem describes a possible understanding of the interplay between finite and Infinite:

I am a Point of Light

> I am a point of Light
>
> I invite other points of Light to join with me to expand Light and Awareness.
>
> I look to the All to provide the synchronous rhythm to carry us forward.
>
> I delight in expanding connections throughout the Universe.
>
> I am abundantly aware of many things happening simultaneously within the matrix of the Great Being, the Great Being of which I am a part.

My point of Light can expand to embrace the All where answers a ever forthcoming.

My point of Light can stay small if I wish so that I experience the full impact of the infinite variety of finite awareness.

Either way, the rhythm and being-ness of the All is enhanced.

The Symphonic Sound is rich and varied.

I am Love and Love is me.

Love is the ongoing Song that sings through the Infinite and the finite.

We are ONE.

The poem can be helpful for people to explore relating to the Mystery in this way to counter the belief that humans are unredeemable and heaven is unattainable. Rising up from such a lowly place feels impossible. If, however, we have a more lateral relationship, everything feels not only more possible but zestfully intriguing. We become two sides of one coin with the communication between providing the impetus for change and growth.

Notice that this poem expresses the fact that Infinite and infinite variety of finite awareness, continue on parallel paths. The change in relating comes then with conscious awareness when one chooses to step onto a different path.

We in the Western world have explored finite awareness with extreme precision. While we are prepared for amazing careers, we are not prepared for many life circumstances and certainly not death passage. The incredible suffering that people experience during times of transition to the Greater World should alert us to this sad fact. Having a conversation with Divine Essence changes the way we perceive death passage. We move from a very narrow perspective to a more vast perspective, which results in the loving and caring for which we all yearn. We come to understand the idea of spiritual birth.

An Arc of Energy

For a visual representation, one might draw an interrupted continuum from Exploration of Finite through Infinite Variety at one end to Exploration of Infinite Vastness on the other. Drawing an arc from finite to Infinite energetically defines the space in which a conversation with Spirit takes place and is on a newly created path opening to new experiences.

Likewise, in creating a new production, the performing artist is stepping on to this path. S/he declares the intention to open to the wisdom of the Vastness. Likewise, the author, the mystic, and the poet each set an intention for the project and each intends to engage the Mystery. Each also expects an infusion of energy greater than hers or his alone.

When a person is making a death transition, that person opens to the wisdom of the Mystery. Consciousness shifts dramatically as the vibrations intermingle and expand. When Grandma talks of seeing her sister, Aunt Mary, who passed five years ago, we accept this as fact and celebrate the opening to seeing for this passing elder. When my father told me he was going to "live with God" he was in the knowing. If we can see through these eyes, we understand mystical energies are moving. The soul crossing is infused with energies greater than his or hers alone.

Imagine multitudes of paths—each creating new arcs. This represents an infusion of new ideas from many different souls that are creating an electrifying source of energy, change and growth. Finite and Infinite are working together to create ever new energetic solutions to problems and answers to dreams.

Reflecting as Communication

Another way to think about communication as energy is envisioning it as a process of reflection back and forth between finite and Infinite, human and Divine. Imagine a small circle representing the soul inside a much larger circle representing the Infinite. The sea between is the place of communication as each sends energetic messages to the other.

Considering this illustration helps to visually represent how we can receive messages through many forms. We ask Spirit a question, and then we keep ourselves alert for an answer. Spirit reflects back to us the answer. A communication from Spirit can come in any form quite literally. An answer to a question might be a person knocking on our door; it might be a dream; it might be a song. Also, answers might come immediately or may take months. The important thing to realize is that we must remain vigilant in our awareness because these answers are often subtle. They only begin to seem obvious after we have practiced listening and have learned the language of the subtle world.

Center Point Grid

Another possible way to perceive this creative journey is through looking at holding the energetic center as in the Center Point Grid. Zero is the desired place from which to operate. Each numeric representation has its own perspective, which can pull us off center. To come to balance, we need to keep our energetic awareness towards the zero at center. The grid helps to remind us of when we have moved out of alignment.

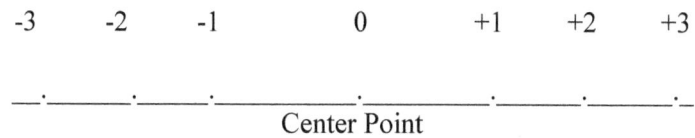

From the performing arts perspective, in dance we speak of moving from our center. This center is often imagined by envisioning a thread going from the heavens through the core our bodies and into earth. Moving from this awareness and concentrating on spotting allows us to execute beautiful pirouettes without falling.

Similarly, when walking someone across the threshold, if we stay at the energetic center, we are able to complete the task with balance and awareness. Holding the center at the space between worlds, we can see a wide spectrum including this world and the Greater World. Once this process is internalized, it is easier to hold center when involved in a death passage. Anything that tries to pull us away from his place of awareness is not allowed to interrupt our focus.

Understanding Vibration

Understanding vibration is a key point in comprehending how such conversations can occur. Everything is made of vibration. Earth is a very dense vibration. The Higher Realms are much lighter and much more subtle. The path between these is a continuum of changing frequencies from dense to light. Death passage is an expansion, which requires souls to move sequentially through lighter and lighter frequencies. This is a natural process, which changes one's conscious awareness. Thus, death from this perspective is a change in frequency or vibration.

Similarly, beings from other realms vibrate at different frequencies as a part of the Cosmic Symphony. When we vibrate at a frequency within their range, we can see and hear each other. If one wishes to change one's operating frequency while on earth, one can embark on a deep meditation practice, take yoga, or work with breathing into the heart, or work with sound healing.

Communication with Subtle Realms while on Earth

Opening our awareness to the different realms that surround us in everyday life is an excellent way to practice skills necessary to be present for death passage. Practicing with these subtle vibrations is often easier than at the time of death passage because there isn't the tremendous emotional challenge. Beings in the subtle realms are very much interested in a collaborative journey and they very lovingly respond. It is not that they constantly chatter like we do but that our communications can intersect at important times. Through the techniques of releasing, deepening and expanding, and using creative process and meditative focus, we become one with the space between when engaging this energy. This is the same type of energetic change with which we appear to be engaging throughout the process of death passage.

Communicating with the subtle aspects of the Mystery is a very creative and dynamic process. This improvisation is always fresh, new and alive. The moment-to-moment sequence of events keeps us riveted and challenged in ways that we are never challenged in everyday life. Yet, the wisdom gleaned readily applies to situations in our daily lives.

Earth Mother

To begin understanding opening to subtle realms Native American Spirituality is an amazing resource. Native people see all beings as living beings including Earth Mother.

Dhyani Ywahoo, of the Cherokee nation, shares this beautiful visualization to assist in connecting with Earth Mother:

> Subtle communication begins in the heart, in your affirmation of resonance with the clear light essence within yourself and all beings. Visualize the three fires burning in the sacrum—will, compassion, active mind—and see the two

spirals of light dancing in your spine, sun, and moon, mother and father.

At the heart center visualize the two triangles, apex to apex, and sense above the head the seven stars, seven gateways of subtle knowing, whence cascades purifying rainbow light, vivifying your body and mind. Sitting in the light, allow a vision of peace to arise in the mind's eye of your heart. See yourself and your relatives peaceful, your co-workers and community, your neighborhood and extended family, your nation and planet. How would it look, how would it feel, how would it be, the world peaceful, all beings at peace, all needs fulfilled in harmony, all resources of Earth appreciated and returned through the gifts of the people? In your heart see the generosity and see Mother Earth giving abundantly that all may eat. Feel yourself as clear, flowing water, the waters that may be renewed. Contemplate this beauteous vision; let it infuse and permeate your mind.

Now, from your heart, from the heart of this peaceful vision, send a beam of light to the very heart of Earth, and communicate upon that beam of light your radiant vision of a peaceful people, peaceful planet. Communicate to Mother Earth her children's dream of love and harmony that it may manifest for all beings in all worlds. Three times send the message of peace out along the heart's ray of light to the crystal heart of Earth; then pause. Await the returning pulse. Feel the energy, acknowledge communion. Recognize, acknowledge the relationship of thought. Rest awhile in happy communion, dreaming with Earth a dream of peace. In closing, draw light beam back into heart, draw all energies into the light spiral in your spine. Give thanks. It is good.

When I first experienced this process I was amazed to receive the returning beam of light straight into my heart. It was pure, loving and powerful. This type of communication opens us to understanding the larger sphere of awareness which our loved ones preparing to transition to the Greater World are also learning.

Nature Spirits

Nature spirits are very closely intertwined with our lives and us. When we can open to seeing and hearing these beautiful beings, they are wonderful companions on the journey. They can see things that we do not understand and happily share their knowledge with us.

The Findhorn Community has applied this type of collaborative effort to develop astounding gardens in Scotland. When gardening, try asking a nature spirit a question for which you do not have the answer. The reply will surprise and delight you.

Chanting is a beautiful approach to help us center and connect with subtle realms. The Heart Chant, from Dhyani Ywahoo, is an excellent way to express our deep love. I first heard this chant when Dhyani spoke in Boulder. She explained that this is an expression of love. English only has one word for love and it so often feels inadequate. Chanting the Heart Chant brings a depth into the expression of love that far surpasses the limitations of the English language:

> *Ah, Ah, Ah*
> *Ah, Ah, Ah, Ah*
> *(Repeat)*
> *Ah tesh na he, na*
> *Ah tesh na he, na*
> *Ah ni qo qo ne, ah ne qo ne*
> *Tesh na, ha ha*
> *Tesh na, ha ha*

As one begins to learn to open to subtle energies this chant is a good starting point because nature spirits respond very sweetly and directly. To begin, think about an aspect of nature, which makes your heart sing. If it is wild flowers, sing the Heart Chant sitting in a meadow of wildflowers every day until a response is received. If it is rock beings then sit on the same rock outcropping and sing the Heart Chant. Await response by using the creative process techniques of listening, allowing, and unfolding. Use journaling to track all that you hear and feel. Once one experiences this two way communication, one begins to actually understand the living essence of the All.

In December of 2004 my daughter and I purchased a stunning live blue spruce tree in a pot for our Christmas celebration in Santa Fe. I told the tree at the time that we were moving back to Colorado and we would plant her in the high mountains where a blue spruce could thrive. In December of 2010 the tree was still in the pot in front of our house. I felt guilty for not keeping my promise. I walked towards the tree one evening at dusk and told her how badly I feel about not caring for her properly. Her response was astounding:

"It is my deep honor to light the way for the Christ child."

This little tree was the only tree to have Christmas lights each year. We looked forward to the beauty she cast as she welcomed us home in the cold and snow in the dark, which she had been doing for seven years now. She has had a good life. All is well.

Likewise, years ago I had a geranium plant in the house that I thought needed trimming. When I inquired if she would like that, to my surprise she said no. In fact, she kept saying no until she was twenty feet tall reaching towards the peak of the A-frame house.

In working with death passage I always sing to the departing soul. The Heart Chant is one chant I use frequently. It has always been both deepening and expanding for souls crossing the threshold regardless of the language barrier. Holding energetic center is critical as is feeling comfortable with communicating with other realms.

Pets

Animal lovers are all certain that pets have important things to say. Connecting with them telepathically is a wonderful way to practice the skill and opens doors to a very interesting relationship. When I am able to connect with my pets, I often receive pictures as in the following example.

> Our cat Pierre was gone for many days. I was beside myself with concern for his well-being. I called and called to no avail. Finally, when I thought I could bear it no more, I received two pictures in my meditation. The first picture showed me that he was injured and hiding in rock outcropping to be safe from predators. The second showed a deer caring for him. The love between the deer and the cat was beautiful. Two days later, Pierre returned home, injured and limping, but ok.

I have also received words from a pet. When my cat Felice was just one year old she wanted to sprout her independence and went off on a trek. Four days was a long time for such a tiny one to be out in the wild of the forest. When I finally connected with her she said, "I come bringing greetings." The next day she returned happy and healthy.

Our cat Shadow Music was killed suddenly in year 2015. As a kitten, she insisted from the very beginning that she would not, under any circumstances, consider being an indoor pet. She would in fact destroy such a house. So, of course, I complied! She lived for eight years coming and going at all hours in a forest setting. This, she felt, was a wonderful accomplishment!

The days following her disappearance, I was agonizing until I heard the Halleluiah Chorus on the radio in the middle of July. This was her favorite song. When I came home after work, we would skip through the house with this music playing while she chased the ribbon I was dangling. That night, she brought the Halleluiah Chorus again just in case I hadn't noticed. Finally, I checked on the Other Side. She came running up to me and said, "Look what I can do!" She was growing large as the sky and then returning to her normal size. This is something one can only do on the Other Side. Remember Georgiana as I was descending the stairs, and Pricilla when she returned to say thank you? Thus, while I did not wish for Shadow Music to be gone from here, I was settled in knowing that she made her way to my soul's care.

In these examples, I am inquiring about the well-being of another. I am opening to the wisdom of Vastness. Also, I am listening, allowing, unfolding. Something new is being created. Throughout a death passage telepathic communication is the most natural thing in the world. It is fluid and simple. Once we connect energetically, the conversation happens. We do not have to "make" it happen. Our souls know this realm well.

Communicating with One's Soul and with Angelic Realms

One's Own Soul

As skills in listening improve we can focus on having this interchange with our soul. While we can also start at this juncture, it is sometimes difficult to discern the answers. Interestingly, once we have gotten feedback from Earth Mother, nature spirits or pets, it is easier to recognize answers from our soul.

Communicating with the soul is wondrous journey. Our soul guidance comes from the connection with higher spiritual realms and is very insightful. To connect with the soul, undertaking a meditation practice, yoga or walking the labyrinth helps us live from a more centered point of view. Select a practice, which feels deep and heartfelt. Techniques such as applied kinesiology or the pendulum also can assist in soul knowledge as can studying the I-Ching. There are many approaches for each of these and all are highly developed skills, which take time to learn. If time is of the essence, try to find someone already trained to assist. Basic information, like learning the soul name, can be an important step in expanding perception.

Once familiar with the process, we can ask our soul a question and use creative process in listening for the answer. A soul's answers can come in any form. Be alert for dreams and communication through meditation as well as thoughts as immediate feedback.

Soul Perspective:
Being in communication with the current form is a soul's great joy. Working together brings a new vibration into existence which opens many doors.

When I began to work on this book I inquired of my soul each day for a month to gain an understanding of her perspective on death passage and Soul Passage Midwifery.

Soul Perspective:
Soul Passage Midwives lovingly work with thoughts, intentions, fears, energies, Universal Laws, perceptions. They connect with souls in need of assistance when entering or leaving through portal ways. In death passage, often on earth now the personality has no awareness of the soul, thus the terror is stark and real. To have to learn to trust this process and to transition all at the same time is a large task indeed.

A Soul Passage Midwife can assist the personality and soul to have this conversation prior to death passage so that the soul goes forward in strength to the appropriate place and the personality is spared upheaval and terror. When separation of the ego occurs, the person is aligned with the soul and simply feels the fading of a part no longer

> *necessary, as in putting away childhood toys. The joy and ecstasy of merging with the soul is a beautiful and powerful experience. It proceeds like positive growth moving forward with the continuum of universal life stages.*

Once the doors are open to communicating with the Soul, there are no limits on the avenues available for sharing a message. We begin to expect the unexpected, yet never know for certain exactly what that will entail.

Soul to Angel Communication

The experiences contained in the preceding chapters are all examples of soul to soul to soul communication. This expanded awareness makes our lives larger, richer and in harmony with the natural order. These encounters are based on universal law, not on any man made pronouncements. Souls understand this intuitively. Interestingly, practicing connecting with angels while on earth makes connecting with other souls easier.

Spiritual beings of all kinds and angels specifically are very much attuned to serving earth people. They work on our behalf whether we realize it or not and respond to requests whether we realize it or not. One critical requirement is clarity of the request. If we are not clear, the answer we are seeking may not be forthcoming because we do not recognize the response as such.

When I first began asking angels I did not know which one to invoke so I invited all of them. They are very willing to infuse any step with energy where we feel uncertain. Often I also simply ask that they send whoever can be of most help at the time. Through the years, certain angels have been consistently present because of the focus of my work with death passage.

The responses experienced with Earth Mother, nature spirits, and pets are similar subtle messages as are those experienced with the angels. Start with the natural inclination, which has already been practiced, then try different ways to expand abilities. Repeating the process is what develops skill. Keep a journal to help understand personal preferences and ways of working which feel natural as well as those, which are successful. There is more than one correct approach!

Believing is the other part of the equation. The mind tries to discount all of these conversations because it wants to be in charge. Once we understand the antics of the mind, they cease to have such importance. We begin listening to more subtle messages and charting a much larger course. Then believing becomes knowing through experience and the mind not only realizes its rightful place, but also we realize its rightful place.

Recognizing an answer from an angel takes practice with creative process in listening, allowing, unfolding, and having a conversation. The responses are always loving in nature and can come through words, feelings, visual pictures, knowing (an "ah ha" moment). The list is endless. I have had clouds form in the sky as an answer to a pressing question. Divination cards have helped many people in this regard. Please practice listening daily, to give an avenue for receiving responses. Once practiced, conversing with angels becomes as natural as any other conversation. This becomes a beautiful way of life.

Archangel Sandalphon:
Open the heart to remember the abundant assistance. Our mission is to help the knowing and ease the way. Learn this lesson well. Act upon an insight with genuine caring.

Archangel Sandalphon assures us of the genuine assistance from the angels. They wish to help the knowing, which opens us to the wonders of the subtle realms and the ways of the Higher Realms. This, they believe, is to help ease the way. Their love for humanity is ever enduring and thoughtful. Archangel Sandalphon cautions us to act with genuine caring.

Archangel Azreal:
Marked change invites our intercession. Death passage appears as an energetic fountain. When wishing to direct the movement of energy, come to clear knowing before acting.

Archangel Azreal shares that angels know of an impending passage because of the energetic change in the frequency, appearing as an energetic fountain, inviting their intercession. If we are to be involved, Archangel Azreal cautions that we must be in the place of clear knowing and clarity before acting.

When my mother was making her transition, I was surprised but thrilled when I first encountered the angels. They help all transitioning souls; we can rest in that knowledge. Remember the angels helping Corrine and Lisa? Remember their assistance with Gabrielle? Their message is that they are available to help everyone at the time of a transition. That includes you. Simply take the time to invite them if you wish for their assistance.

To request assistance from an angelic presence try the following process:

Request for Angelic assistance

>Archangel Jophiel, I honor you and bless you
>I invite you into my heart
>Chant the Heart Chant or other chant
>My question today is:
>Await the answer using the steps in creative process.
>Listening, allowing, unfolding, improvisation
>Record the question and answer in a journal.
>Give thanks
>Ask another question or act on the information given
>Give thanks, close the session.

To continue the conversation once it begins we must act on the information received or ask another question. This can feel a little challenging at times. Yet, if we are going to work with Spiritual Beings, we need to incorporate their advice into our world. One reason for keeping a journal of our questions and answers is to help us recognize that we are having an actual conversation.

Gleaning Understanding:

Energetically, we live in a continuum of frequencies moving from dense to fine and finer. Once this is understood, it is easy to see life in its myriad of forms. There is nothing scary about this awareness. Loss of the feminine principle simply has darkly colored the expression of the larger and very beautiful aspects of subtle realms. This can be regained through deliberate effort in communicating with Spirit. Practicing with Earth Mother, nature spirits, and pets is an ever-available avenue while living on earth. Likewise, deliberately placing the attention on the Higher Realms of the individual soul, soul to soul communication and soul to Angelic Realm communication opens doors long shut.

Insights for Those Preparing to Cross Over:
- Take time to practice communicating with nature spirits or pets while on earth. This communication uses the same part of the intelligence and one's awareness as is used for crossing the threshold.
- Make the effort to communicate with angels. They help all souls crossing the threshold.
- See if you can connect with your own soul through breathing into your heart.

Insights for Families and Professionals:
- Become comfortable with telepathic communication. This alone will help when the loved one is crossing over. You

will not have to waste time wondering if it is true. Practice in nature while you are here on earth.
- If you have a pet that is near death, take time to work with conscious awareness in your effort. Pets respond readily.

Conclusion

As we open to trying to understand how to communicate with the Mystery and practice bringing this awareness into our experience, gentleness moves into our lives and many beliefs, which create limitation, are lifted. A simplicity for which we have yearned opens to greet our hearts no matter the franticness of our society. Simultaneously, our world expands exponentially bringing the wondrous into our lives. Particularly at the time of a death passage, this is a very welcome occurrence.

Part III:

Personal Application

We are each day, each moment, learning to die: to dissolve into the ocean of pure being.

Stephen Levine, (*Who Dies?*)

Chapter Nine
Living Tapestry of Light

Creating a Living Tapestry of Light is entering the experience of a death transition in a sacred manner. You are embracing the calling forth of the soul who is a sacred being. This way of entering sets the correct tone, creates space for Spirit to participate, and allows souls to connect with one another. Each person preparing to cross will move to a different rhythm and create a unique crossing. Each family's expression will be different. Know that there are no mistakes. There are plans, which may change in the challenge of the moment. Be gentle with yourself and your family.

From the soul perspective, this transition is a beautiful celebration. Honoring the soul at this juncture keeps the Light at the forefront of the situation consistently. Entering in this way holds the correct vibration for the loved one and the family. While each celebration will vary according to the time available, people involved, location and desires of the loved one passing, the basic principles remain the same for everyone. For families and the loved one, simplicity is the best approach. Select those prayers, practices, songs and chants, which feel within reach of everyone at a difficult time.

FOR THOSE PREPARING TO CROSS OVER

This is the Great Change. You have a lifetime of wisdom, which has prepared you for this moment. Know that your soul is ready. Try to think of the process as an adventure to be encountered with curiosity. I know this sounds challenging but moving through in this way helps to create a peaceful transition. There is learning and remembering moment by moment. If it is the eleventh hour, invite Spirit to assist with a simple prayer and welcome the assistance. Know that you are in the best hands in the Spirit realms. Step through each experience deliberately focusing on the Light.

If there is time, think about the process of death as a process of Releasing, Deepening and Expanding as explained in Chapter Four in this book. You are letting go of the body to embrace your expanded soul awareness. This is a beautiful process. You are letting go of outmoded beliefs to welcome new perspectives, which better serve you when in the form of a soul or core essence. You are growing in astounding ways. You are remembering things forgotten for a time. This is an exhilarating process. You are embracing the precise frequency that allows for you to cross over gently. Spirit Beings are ever present to assist you in welcoming this frequency as your new expression.

Receptive Practices:
Think of breath, heart and soul as creating the path inward for you to follow.

Breath: Breath is your anchor for as long as you are in the body. Simply observe the breath going in and out. This focus takes concentration, which is something very much needed for the upcoming journey. Daily practice brings familiarity, which brings ease into focusing when the time draws near, regardless of challenges of the physical body.

Heart: Breathing in to your heart is the next step on the path before you. Your heart is a wise and gentle being that connects with your soul. Its intelligence is opened and expanded simply by breathing into it.

Soul: This being you will undoubtedly recognize as your true self. Welcome Home! This eternal aspect of you knows the Greater World well. She or he has not forgotten. The core of your being is held in tact through all the trials and tribulations of a temporary earth sojourn.

Expressive Practices:
Word/Chant

Create one word or short chant to speak at the time of your transition. This is a loving message shared at a profound moment. The word or simple chant will have great meaning to you personally and therefore, deep meaning to those in the Greater World. This is only for your ears. Do not share it with anyone. Change it as many times as you like until you feel certain it is your deepest expression, then silently practice it daily.

Prayer/Poem/Song/Chant

Create a prayer, a poem, a song or a chant to be read and/or sung as you are transitioning. Have family members help you and/or give this to family when you feel it is ready so they can practice. When you hear this prayer, poem, song or chant as you are transitioning, you will know that you are actually in the midst of the Great Change. You can also ask family to read or sing traditional family favorites if you prefer.

If you have the energy to create an outline of what your wishes are for the actual transition time, please take the time to do so. The other chapters in this book can help guide your creation. Family members will very much appreciate knowing that they are honoring your wishes and that will give them strength to keep moving forward. It is a beautiful gift to share with each other.

FOR FAMILIES AND PROFESSIONALS

Creating a sacred farewell at the bedside is something that all families can do if they wish, but it is helpful if it is prepared ahead of time. The tremendous value in doing so is that this focus brings everyone together for a higher purpose and assists the loved one to have a most beautiful send off. Holding the Presence for a loved one helps uplift the frequencies for a graceful passage. It keeps the family riveted towards conscious awareness and holds less harmonious thoughts and actions at bay. Discord at the time of death can and does often tear families apart. That is reason alone for negotiating this time in life in a different way. Expanding awareness offers the antidote to chaotic thinking and feeling. If the family doesn't feel prepared to do this on their own, then inviting a Soul Passage Midwife is recommended.

Even if you feel prepared to move through the process with this perspective, there will be times of faltering, of outrage, of sheer exhaustion from the seeming insanity of it all. Take space for yourself, cry, pound on the pillows, and know that it is all a temporary part of the journey. Be gentle with yourselves. Return when you are able.

Creating a Living Tapestry of Light
This is a precious moment in a soul's journey. Creating a Living Tapestry of Light honors the soul at every juncture. The time of a soul passage is a time of outpouring of Love from the Higher Realms and from people surrounding the person crossing. This is truly a cosmic gathering and celebration. It is a coming together of Beings from the Higher Realms and people on earth to form a sacred circle for the passage. Each side of the veil holds one half of the circle with the person crossing creating the bridge between. Radiant Light, of course, infuses the entire circle. Envisioning the preparations as a part of this endeavor brings deep purpose to a most sacred moment. Also, thinking of the passing from this perspective calls forth the soul or core essence. Seeing through these eyes helps uplift the vibration for everyone.

Labyrinth

When first realizing a loved one may pass, walk the labyrinth and offer a prayer that the soul have a gentle transition. Use this sacred tool throughout the process to help uplift the frequencies for the loved one and the family. Try to find a time to do this walking meditation with the entire family to offer a prayer together for the loved one crossing.

Walking the labyrinth offers the opportunity for the family to move together in a sacred environment with shared purpose. The design of the labyrinth is based on sacred geometry so it helps to expand and uplift each person without the encumbrance of words. It is a walking meditation. With the entire family at the center of the labyrinth, offer a heartfelt prayer for Spirit to ease the way for the loved one crossing and the family.

Nature

Creating time for a walk in nature together is also a positive practice. This is uplifting and deeply nurturing. Nature is very present when people are grieving. Focus on noticing the great beauty of nature and taking that in to soothe your aching heart.

Sacred Space

Creating a sacred environment helps the loved one passing and helps the family. A sacred space can be created anywhere. It infuses the surroundings with higher vibrations to help hold the focus and bring ease to the crossing. There are many ways of doing this, so please adapt all suggestions to the situation at hand.

Tea lights, candles, mini-strings of lights, flowers, wall hangings, artwork, and photos can all be displayed to create a soft, nurturing, sacred environment. Someone who is passing requires softness in the surroundings. Spraying the environment with the essential oil of rose clears the space and uplifts the frequency. Be creative and think of this process as a gift to the departing loved one.

Altar

An altar gives a focus for families to participate in the preparation for the journey. Prayer sets the tone and the correct frequency. This practice establishes energetic connections between families and the loved one, between the loved one and Spirit, and between families and Spirit.

Placed by the bedside, the altar can have teddy bears, seashells, pictures, crystals, candles, or whatever the family wishes to share with the person departing. Children love to bring in artwork to place on the altar for Grandma. Just as it gives them a sense of participation, it also gives adults a sense of purpose. Adults often bring a flower to place on the altar or a heartfelt prayer unless the family has a stated theme.

Prayer Basket

A prayer basket specifically holds prayers for the loved one. These prayers are living symbols that can accompany the loved one across the threshold. Collecting them in the basket to be read at the time of the crossing is a beautiful expression and gift for the loved one. The prayers can be private as well. Use prayer as the foundation rather than as an afterthought. This secures the correct frequency and tone.

The prayer basket can be made of wicker, pottery, glass, crystal, abalone shells, china, or any container of special significance in the heart of the person crossing or family. Have small cards with envelopes available for visitors. Making the cards can be a family project to bring children and adults together. Following the passing, the prayers are burned and released in sacred ceremony.

Vibrational Canoe

The vibrational canoe is made of prayer, poetry, and/or song. These can be original and created by the family or favorites that are familiar to everyone. The building of this energetic canoe by the family brings a focus of positive expression, which can be included in the sacred ceremony. The caution here is to keep everything simple. Short prayers and poems are easier to read with tears in the eyes. Singing a simple song many times is easier than trying to remember many verses. The importance here is for the one passing to feel the genuine love. These heartfelt words and music travel with the loved one across the threshold.

Shawl of Comfort

Weaving a shawl of comfort is to assist the family through the journey, which of course extends to the loved one crossing over. Each family member needs to feel supported and loved throughout the process. Each is grieving, in his or her, own way. It is not an easy task to maintain one's balance through such a challenging time.

Knowing that the other family members are holding each person in strength is a powerful energetic statement.

Looking for ways to be thoughtful of one another by asking what would make each person feel uplifted is another beautiful expression to bring forward. Consciously weave these requests into your schedule knowing that it will create a loving environment for each person to move through the experience.

Song

Singing provides a constant secure thread in the midst of the chaos of dramatic change. Families can play a vital role here by choosing something simple to sing while the loved one is in the process of the Great Change. Know that your loved one hears your voices. Another option is to play a soothing piece on an instrument.

Sacred Ceremony

Creating sacred ceremony is something beautiful to do together as a family. Keep the process simple and doable. This ceremony takes place at the bedside as the loved one is preparing to pass. When it is clear that the loved one will pass soon, the family begins the ceremony. Thus, the focus becomes being present with the loved one in a sacred manner rather than waiting for the crossing to be over with.

Everyone who wishes to take part in the sacred ceremony has an important role, which can include prayer reader, song leader, candle lighter, bell ringer, altar caretaker, space designer. The preparations are simple and joyful. This focus offers the opportunity to place the attention on the celebratory aspects of the passing while working together. If someone falters from the enormity of the emotional challenge, someone else steps forward to assist. There is no judgment. Each is helping each in the thick of the challenge.

Sample Ceremony

- ~ Spraying of Rose Water made of essential oil to purify the space
- ~ Lighting of Candle on the altar~ Offering the Prayer of Invitation for Spirit Holding the Presence
- ~ Song or Chant
- ~ Placing of Heather flower essence on the wrists of the loved one.
- ~ Placing Frankincense Essential Oil on the forehead of the loved one
- ~ Prayer(s) from the prayer basket or sacred tradition
- ~ Poem
- ~ Song or Chant
- ~ Ringing of Bell
- ~ Thanking of Spirit for all assistance
- ~ Blowing out candle.

Note

If there is time and you feel you would like to go more deeply before the soul crosses the threshold, go through Chapters 4-8 to select practices which feel doable for you. Do not worry about things which are not possible. Keep your attention on that which is possible.

Also look at Stepping Stones for Families in the following Soul Passage Midwife section in this Chapter to see if that material feels helpful.

FOR THE SOUL PASSAGE MIDWIFE

Personal application for Soul Passage Midwifery is a quiet, subtle work of removing resistances and opening the heart through continuous softening. Spirit advises and directs. Souls work harmoniously with other souls within the symphony of the All. We do not leave our bodies; rather, we expand until everything is happening within our sphere of awareness. Energy can be sent anywhere within this sphere. We are in our bodies and in the expanded realms simultaneously. We quiet our thoughts. We quiet our needs. We quiet our judgments. Love is everywhere in an unbounded state. We are in service to Love expressing Life.

Like a spiral of expansion, life here on earth and life in the Higher Realms moves continuously seeking ever-new awareness. Within each domain there is always room for growth. A foot in each world, conscious awareness is constantly weaving them together. As a Soul Passage Midwife, each aspect is held with equanimity. Rather than either/or, the movement is for the whole.

Opening to Soul Passage Midwifery is a study of a different nature. There are no time tables. Spirit gives the diploma. One can work and travel into the Unseen realms with a Soul Passage Midwife or souls interested can begin at home by practicing the awarenesses presented in the this book. Divine Forces are ever ready to assist so there is every reason to begin now. If time is short, breathe into the heart, offer the Prayer of Invitation inviting Spirit to assist in Holding the Presence, and know that Spirit is there on every level to help. I believe that it is the natural order for a family member to accompany the loved one across the threshold and return to share the description of the passage with the family. In this way, families are prepared and can pass the information along to future generations. Thus I encourage families to be as involved as possible.

In creating the Living Tapestry of Light, the Soul Passage Midwife is a weaver of worlds. She interconnects the soul who is crossing, the family, and the beings in the Great Beyond. This Cosmic gathering is a powerful moment. Holding the Presence is the conscious awareness that ties it all together. Each of the tools described below are used artistically, when needed, and function within the context of Holding the Presence. The Soul Passage Midwife selects from the artist's palette just the right color and just the right frequency to assist the soul crossing.

Receptive Elements
The preceding chapters have focused on the receptive elements precisely because this is the awareness that allows one to move with unwavering steadfastness through the course of crossing the threshold. The Soul Passage Midwife practices and utilizes the following elements at all times.

Releasing, Deepening, Expanding

In preparing to expand, one releases all preconceived ideas and comes to a place of intrigue or inviting new awareness. One moves into the heart and prepares to pray for another with deep love and caring.

Holding the Presence

Holding the Presence from Swami Yogananda, is the container for the entire process. Envision the nesting of Spirit and matter. Offer a Prayer of Invitation for Spirit to assist in Holding the Presence. Holding the self in the higher vibration, one does not allow lower thought discord to intrude.

Become familiar with the techniques of each of the Archangels' recommendations in Chapter 5 so that they are accessible at a moment's notice. Each angel offers a unique voice to embrace at the time of a death transition.

Meditative Focus

The mind needs direction. One holds a meditative focus daily to help clear the mind and calm the emotions. To keep thoughts from wandering, select a single focus such as, "I look with wonder, awe and reverence to the Sustaining Presence of my life and all life." Use other meditation examples contained in this book or write several of your own to have ready.

Creative Process

Through creative process, one is available for conscious awareness as it presents itself moment by moment. We are open to listening, allowing, unfolding and improvisation. As information is received, it is acknowledged. The Soul Passage Midwife then asks another question or acts on the information received. This process requires deep focus.

Interdimensional Communication

The focus is on both receptive and expressive language simultaneously for this communication, so one states prayers simply and remains open to receiving messages from Spirit, from the soul preparing to cross, from one's own soul.

Expressive Elements

The expressive elements are a natural outpouring resulting from the awareness attained from the deep internal search of the receptive elements. These are the same elements Families can use as explained earlier, but with several additions specific to the Soul Passage Midwife.

Labyrinth

Use the labyrinth as an essential part of the process from beginning to end. Walk the labyrinth yourself to offer prayers for the loved one and family. Invite the family to walk the labyrinth as a special walking meditation together. At the center, join together to offer a prayer for the loved one crossing.

Nature

Nature is used for solace, comfort and inspiration. If there is not a labyrinth available, make sure to take the family out in nature. This could be as simple as going outside and sitting under a tree, or taking a short walk in the neighborhood. Help the family notice the profound beauty that emanates from nature.

Sacred Space

Creating a sacred space is an essential component for the work of the Soul Passage Midwife. This is kept in the home. Candles, incense, essential oils, and tones all evoke warmth as well as purifying the energy in the space. The quality of peace is the environment that helps calm the emotions, as well as clearing the mind and allowing Spirit to be heard. Choose a space that has a door, which can be closed when someone is passing. Also, if you have to leave, the peaceful container remains intact and can be re-entered quickly upon return.

Active Altar

An active altar in the home of the Soul Passage Midwife is imperative. This is an expressive element letting Spirit know that you are seriously committed to this work. It is used daily to invite Spirit to guide our work.

Place items on the altar that support a high vibration such as crystals, flowers, essential oils and sacred objects. Keep it pure and beautiful. This altar holds prayers in a sacred manner, thus supporting the Soul Passage Midwife in her work.

Prayer Basket

The prayer basket at the home of the Soul Passage Midwife is used to place all prayers for the departing soul. As soon one learns of a passing, the process begins. Light a candle, call on Divine Forces, and state the prayer including the name, city and state of the person preparing to cross. Write this information on a prayer card and place it in the prayer basket. This beautiful sacred object holds radiant prayers offered at a profound moment. Pray each day for all of the souls involved in a passage. This helps energetically to build the bridge of eternity so that when the time is at hand, the soul will pass gently.

Vibrational Canoe

Prayer, song and chant accompany the loved one across the threshold. This is the essence of the vibrational canoe. It is a most loving gift to the departing loved one. Ask the loved one if there is something special that he or she would like to hear during the transition. Ask the family if there are special hymns or songs to include. Create the vibrational canoe out of prayers, songs and chants that have deep meaning to those involved. Collect several of each to have on hand at the critical moment.

Shawl of Comfort

We might also think of this as a shawl of thoughtfulness. Its essence is woven out of the thoughtfulness of family members towards each other and towards the loved one. Speak with each family member to discern a special something that would bring comfort to that person. Help the family to see how they can weave these thoughtful moments into the process of going through each day. You will be surprised at how they uplift each individual and the frequency of the entire process.

Song

Singing is the key that unlocks the window in the heart and connects it energetically with one's own soul, the soul of one passing and with Spirit. This starts with singing to the soul when we first learn of the preparation for passing. It continues daily throughout the preparation and for the entire time of the actual crossing. The Unseen Realms come alive with a majesty that astounds. Our role is to hold the vibration as clearly as we are able and to assist where we are called. Souls are quite familiar with this process so we can trust that they will do what is necessary or call whatever spiritual help is needed. Joseph Rael tells us that singing and chanting are "how we enter into the eternal now." He goes on to explain that, "the energetic vibration of our voices bond us to the spiritual light made of memory, and of now, and of future, for we are the light of universal intelligence. As we chant, the Universe speaks to us in metaphorical images."

Often my songs start simply as a call to the soul crossing, where I offer companionship. This is the best way to connect with the soul. Sing whether in person or long distance. Upon receiving the name, sing and place the name in the prayer basket. Yet, there is no attachment here. We go where we are called. The soul crossing will respond if s/he would like assistance in any way. If not, I know that I have offered a beautiful prayer for a kindred spirit. Perhaps that is all that is needed.

Creating Sacred Ceremony

As a weaver of worlds, you will be intimately involved with the loved one and the family. Help the loved one to discern whether he or she can focus on breath, heart, and soul. Step through this process together to practice daily. Also, ask if the loved one is interested in prayer, chant, or song. If yes, find something that is especially meaningful to that person. If not, the family will care for this in the sacred ceremony. Share any information with the family and ask their guidance in bringing forth the requests of the loved one.

The family will undoubtedly know many things about the loved one that the loved one may not be able to remember or have any interest at this point. Ask the family preferences for the ceremony then help them to carry out their wishes in concert with the wishes of the loved one. Consider that they are under difficult circumstances and try to relieve the burden each step of the way. Ask them to read the sample ceremony and add any special moments that would be meaningful to them. Help them to be as involved as possible. Become adept with improvisation so you can step in as needed at the appointed hour. There may be a world of difference in how a family feels today and how they feel at the time of the transition.

Different Entry Point for Families

If the family is not ready for the Living Tapestry of Light, I suggest the following as a preparation for that process. Facing the unknown, while terrifying on one level, offers the supreme opportunity for expansion. Thus, the option to go through the passage with a different set of parameters and create a different outcome is inherent in the experience from the onset. Of course, this observation immediately brings reaction from the left-brain mindset. To get around this dilemma, families need to enter from an unusual perspective.

Stepping Stones to Help Families

As a first step, read the following words:

>*Opening*
>
>*Embracing*
>
>*Understanding*
>
>*Befriending*
>
>*Cultivating*
>
>*Anchoring*
>
>*Creating*

There is not one word on this list that is threatening in any way. Each word invites possibility. They are stepping stones to help create a map of where one is going in consciousness. Each provides entry into the next level until one arrives at breathing into the heart. Third dimensional things cannot go to the Higher Realms. There is no solace in trying to drag them there. While the above words may seem too light to be of assistance, they are precisely the correct frequency to be able to open conscious awareness to the next level. They rest on the premise of inquiry. Thus, instead of entering the process thinking that one has all of the answers, one enters seeking answers and remaining open to spiritual assistance.

Opening: One accepts not knowing. Not knowing is the cultural dilemma in which we find ourselves. While we do not know, we can learn. In accepting the situation that there is loss of awareness of how to negotiate this time in life, we can commit to opening to create something new. The opportunity to deepen the experience is available.

Embracing: We each have an eternal aspect, core essence, Soul. This eternal aspect remembers how to cross the threshold and is fluid in the ways of the next world. This is key to accepting death as birth. It is the left-brain that assumes and fears annihilation. Since the dominant culture is left-brained, this fear is rampant among citizens. Remembering the existence of the eternal self brings life into the otherwise untenable journey of death.

Understanding: This refers to comprehending that the Universe is a frequency continuum from dense to lighter and lighter. Living on earth is living in a very dense environment. Things appear solid at this density. It is difficult to believe that anything that one cannot see with physical eyes even exists. Yet, other realms do exist at different frequencies. This understanding helps one to move forward to a different perspective of transitioning to the next realm.

Befriending: Befriending Sacred Silence brings Spirit into our midst. Dying is a sacred journey. There is no way around this. We are spiritual beings at our core. The One is ever present in each of us and moves in ways that may not make sense to the mundane world. It is in stillness, in silence, that one connects with this Essence. It moves in ways that are mysterious, and yet, entirely accessible. Taking time for Sacred Silence brings blessed relief to all of the frantic doing, which often erupts at the time of a death passage.

Cultivating: Cultivating conscious awareness is a practice. Human beings learn something new through practice. Until the new awareness becomes second nature, remembering to practice is what must be done. Focusing one's attention in the higher way opens a path, which can be walked again and again. This internal work creates fertile ground for accomplishing external activity with peace.

Anchoring: For the family, anchoring into the awareness of the heart can bring loving awareness into the challenging situation. Actually focusing on breathing into the heart is a key to opening to a higher awareness. This practice is simple and powerful. Once connected, the energies expand automatically bringing uplifting Sacred Feminine frequencies.

Creating: Creating a Living Tapestry of Light at the time of a soul's crossing is a blessed and beautiful task. Awareness of the spiritual journey at hand brings tender leaves of new birth into the midst of the family circle.

Once arriving at this point, families can always choose to go through the practices in Chapters 4-8.

Helping a Soul Across the Threshold

This process is a call to the Celestial Council of Light. The Soul Passage Midwife is a linking energy to invite the process. The Celestial Council of Light responds to all calls for assistance in crossing the threshold. The Divine Feminine presides over each soul passage. This endeavor is not religion specific. Working in this way takes the soul directly to the higher celestial dimensions without the intrusion of lower frequency discord. The Soul Passage Midwife calls on Divine Forces, uses all of the techniques described earlier in the book, and uses intuition and improvisation to assist the soul transitioning.

Steps for the Soul Passage Midwife:
1. Purify the space with Rose Essential Oil.
2. Create an Active Altar if it is not already in place.
3. Light a Candle.
4. Release all preconceived ideas regarding what is about to transpire. Come to center point.
5. Place the name, city, state of the loved one passing in the prayer basket.
6. Breathe into the heart.
7. Offer a Prayer of Invitation to Light Beings to help in Holding the Presence to create a gentle crossing for the soul.
8. Chant *Om* or another sacred chant.
9. Place Heather on the wrists of the loved one. Place Heather in the prayer basket, if long distance.

10. Place Frankincense on the forehead of the loved one, if in person. Place Frankincense in the prayer basket, if long distance.
11. While continuing Holding the Presence, utilize additional techniques including meditative focus, creative process/improvisation and interdimensional communication. Be aware of using each of these practices simultaneously.
12. Focus on the third eye (if you have a meditation practice use this; otherwise skip this step).
13. Sing to the soul crossing while telepathically sending love and offering companionship.
14. Respond to any requests from the soul crossing.
15. Remain alert for receiving auditory, visual or kinesthetic information.
16. Respond intuitively, allowing Spirit to flow through, using creative process techniques of listening, allowing, unfolding, and improvisation.
17. Continue singing for the entirety of the soul passage whether in person or long distance.
18. When complete, thank each Light Being for assistance and bless each.
19. Blow out the candle.
20. Take time for silent reflection.
21. Record all that has transpired in a journal.
22. Create a beautiful translation of the events or keepsake to share with the family.

Gleaning Understanding:

Families and Soul Passage Midwives can be extraordinarily helpful to a soul crossing the threshold. When working with Spirit, that which seems impossible can become a reality. Amazing insights arrive at a moment's notice.

Insights for Those Preparing to Cross Over:
- If you would like to experience death differently than what traditional beliefs have held as standard, make a commitment to trying to have a conscious crossing of the threshold.
- Find time to practice focusing on breath, heart, and soul.
- If you wish to give voice at the time of your passage, practice a song, chant, or prayer.
- If you are able, share any spiritual insights with your family as you go through the process of preparing and transitioning.

Insights for Families and Professionals:
- Preparing for a conscious crossing of the threshold requires a decision from the start. Make this commitment.
- Find time to practice, deliberately focusing your attention on the practices in the preceding pages.
- Cherish the time with your loved one in preparing for this momentous occasion.

Conclusion

The practices in our Western society surrounding death passage beg to be revitalized and understood in a new way. Focusing on the soul and the Higher Realms throughout the process of a transition creates deep purpose to assist during a very challenging time in life. I find that people welcome this focus. It nurtures the souls of the departing one and the family. It brings Light into difficult situations. It brings hope and joy at a time that usually brings despair. As each family brings a unique voice to reweaving this time in life, that voice will be added to weaving great beauty in The Living Tapestry of Light.

Concluding Remarks

The return of the feminine principle brings the uplifting holy frequencies into our midst. This smoothes the path and opens the way for a gentle crossing of the threshold. Delicate, yet profound remembering our birthright brings incredible strength in ways one would not imagine. The constricted reality in which we have been living expands exponentially opening to the wondrous.

The unnatural fear of death actually keeps us trapped in a negative feedback loop of expecting the worst. Knowledge of the actual crossing reveals beauty, welcoming, and celebration. Personal accounts throughout this book demonstrate the extraordinary process of moving through a death passage with conscious awareness. This is possible for each person walking the earth because we come from the Great Beyond. Our souls, or core essence, resonate with this frequency. It is familiar. It is our true nature. We are undoubtedly made of that which lies beyond.

This book is an invitation to see death through different eyes. Approaching conscious dying reveals that souls crossing the threshold, families and Soul Passage Midwives are all experiencing parallel journeys.

While the path is challenging, it can also be intriguing. Entering the experience through deliberately placing the attention offers a precise, moment-by-moment approach to open to conscious dying for each person involved. For those who wish to embark on this profound journey, Radiant Beauty greets each step of the way.

Gleaning understanding from firsthand accounts of a loving family member and a Soul Passage Midwife offers a unique and entirely accessible approach to conscious dying. This intimate look at death invites curiosity and joyous celebration at a time when most people are emotionally paralyzed and grief stricken. From the eternal perspective, the soul perspective, one is simply changing form and continuing on. Conscious awareness is shifting from the person to the soul. This expanded vision brings profound peace.

For those who wish to serve humanity as a Soul Passage Midwife, this is a spiritual practice and a way of life. It is not a standard professional career. One works with Spirit Beings within the Eternal Presence to assist the well-being of another soul. I invite you to explore the Higher Realms to see if it is your calling.

For souls crossing the threshold, I invite you to enter this sacred journey with curiosity. Open your heart to fully embrace the profound gift of eternal life. Make your way moment by moment by listening, allowing and unfolding. Spirit Beings are yearning to assist in whatever way you will let them. May your journey and your welcome be enlightening and uplifting.

In these times, I believe it is critical for each of us to give our highest gift for the collective human consciousness to flower at a higher level. This is my highest gift. I offer it from my heart to families everywhere who feel it unbearable to lose a loved one. This deep pain is deeply etched in every one of us. Please try to remember that each soul, each core essence, is treasured, eternal and that you will see this being again. Of this, I have absolutely no doubt. Once one has the knowing, it cannot be obscured.

Thank you to each reader for considering this perspective. It is an opening into eternal ways that can alter the course of one's life. Thank you to all Spirit Beings who guide this work. Peace.

Epilogue

In these words from Divine Mother, it is apparent that Radiant Beauty finds great joy living in the midst of human awareness. This is an astounding gift. The feminine aspect of each of us can readily understand the preciousness of the love experienced from participating with us, through us, in us, and as us:

Many are the forms I take

    Love the blessed formless drape

        Across the cloudless sea of sky

            Adorning Light, the Joyous I.

Hallowed Halls beckon each

    The ever-forward seeking gaze

        To recognize the One within

            Brilliance as such, I make My Home.

    With, for, through and as Love

            ~Divine Mother

Bibliography

Part I: Across the Veil

Chapter 1: Sight Awakening

>Chapter Quote
>Maria Dancing Heart Hoaglund, *The Most Important Day of Your Life Are You Ready?*, Sedona: Bridge to Dreams Press, 2010, p. 73.

Chapter 2: Sacred Transformation

>Chapter Quote:
>Barbara Brennan, *Hands of Light*, New York: Pleiades Books, 1987, p.69.

Chapter 3: Souls Across the Threshold

>Chapter Quote:
>Jean Houston, *The Search for the Beloved*, New York: Penguin, Putnam Inc., 1987, p. 126.

Part II: Opening to Soul Passage Midwifery

Introduction

>1. C.S. Lewis, *The Complete Chronicles of Narnia, The Lion, the Witch and the Wardrobe*, Great Britain: Harper Collins, 1998, p. 77.
>2. Nancy Wood, "The Rainbow Wood," in *Dancing Moons*, New York: Bantam-Dell Publishing, 1994, p. 77.

Chapter 4: Releasing, Deepening, Expanding

>Chapter Quote:
>Antoine Saint Exupery, *The Little Prince*, Orlando: Harcourt, Inc., p. 70.
>2. Ram Dass, *Still Here*, New York: Riverbend Books, 2000, p.15.

3. Nancy Wood, "Beads of Life," in *Dancing Moons*, New York: Bantam-Dell Publishing, 1994, p. 55.

Chapter 5: Holding the Presence

Chapter Quote:
Parmahansa Yogananda, *Autobiography of a Yogi*, Los Angeles: Self Realization Fellowship, 1946, p. 417.
2. Ibid, p.15.
3. Ibid., p.402.
4. Simeon Nartoomid, http://www.cosmicconsciousnessonline.com/About-Me.html.
5. Sharry Edwards, http://www.soundhealthinc.com/about.html
6. Maia Nartoomid, teaching about Sush Al'Mundra (She Who Lights the World), www.SpiritMythos.org

Chapter 6: Meditative Focus

Chapter Quote:
Soygal Rinpoche, *The Tibetan Book of Living and Dying*, San Francisco: Harper, 1992, p. 20.

Chapter 7: Death Passage as Creative Process

Chapter Quote:
The Findhorn Community, *The Findhorn Garden, Pioneering a New Vision of Man and Nature in Cooperation*, New York: Harper and Row, 1975, opening statement, unnumbered.
2. Soygal Rinpoche, *The Tibetan Book of Living and Dying*, San Francisco: Harper, 1992.

Chapter 8: Interdimensional Communication

Chapter Quote:
Rainbow Eagle, *The Universal Peace Shield of Truths: Ancient American Indian Peace Shield Teachings*, New Mexico: Rainbow Light and Company, 1998, p. 48.

2. Eckhart Tolle, *A New Earth*, New York: Penguin Group, 2005, p. 156.
3. Dr. Lauren Artress, *Walking a Sacred Path, Redicovering the Labyrinth as a Spiritual Tool*, New York: Riverbend Books, 1995, p. 122.
4. Jean Houston, www.jeanhouston.org
5. Barbara Marx Hubbard, www.barbaramarxhubbard.com
6. Maia Nartoomid, www.newearthstar.org
7. Dhyani Ywahoo, *Voices of Our Ancestors*, Boston, MA: Shambhala, 1987, p. 200.
8. Ibid, p. 197.

Part III: Personal Application

Chapter 9: Living Tapestry of Light

Chapter Quote:
Stephen Levine, *Who Dies?*, Garden City: Anchor Books, 1982, p. 271.
2. Joseph Rael, *Being and Vibration*, Tulsa: Council of Oak Books, 1993, p. 118.

About the Author

Patricia L'Dara came to the work of death and dying when her own mother passed twenty-three years ago. Prior to that time, she had never been in a room with anyone crossing the threshold. Death holds within its walls the possibility of utter despair and ecstatic celebration. Patricia deeply experienced the intensity of each, as she looked first through the eyes of a daughter then through the eyes of the soul. From her own encounters with near death, she knew there was nothing to fear but realized helping someone else required a different effort. The initiation with her mom altered the course of her life.

Drawing on her life experience, Patricia finds soul passage to be a deeply engaging interlude containing prayer, creative process, multidimensional awareness, frequency changes and precise meditative focus. Through expanding our understanding of death to include principles familiar to us, Patricia is able to bring unusual clarification to this sacred endeavor. Preparing in advance thus becomes a viable option. Assisting another involves simple steps that families can take.

Patricia's original career focused on higher education. Teaching at a university in Texas, her position included teaching coursework as well as coordinating a federally funded in-service training program in creative arts for people with disabilities. After only two years into her career path, in what seemed a tragic turn of events, catastrophic illness caused her to leave the University. Thus began her search for wholeness.

Traditional Western medicine led to many closed doors and near death. Patricia struggled to find healing. She embraced alternative medicine in its many forms. After a six-year sojourn, she found the experimental research work of Sharry Edwards in BioAcoustics (sound healing). With this technique, her body began to again know quality of life. Understanding life as frequency is a natural outgrowth of this study.

When she was able, she began to go to the dance studio one hour a week to share the joy of dancing with people with disabilities. Over time, this effort blossomed into a nationally recognized performing company, Images in Motion, which was showcased on NBC Nightly

News and in *Parade Magazine*. The Company was featured on Channels 4, 7, and 9 News and in many special interest stories. They performed for the National Dance Association, as well as in theaters and universities. Patricia received the Colorado Dance Book award from the Colorado Dance Alliance and was featured in the book *Unsung Heroes*.

Deep metaphysical study formed a cornerstone of her new path. Along this path, California spiritual healer and teacher, Rev. Joseph Martinez, advised her that she was sick because she was in conflict with her soul direction. Shocked but determined, coming into alignment with her soul preferences became her focus. Some years later, Swami Yogananda promised that if she practiced his Kriya Yoga, she would know her soul and her work. This continues to be her practice today.

Also along the path of healing, Patricia spent many hours alone in the forest. During that time Patricia met and delighted in spending time with nature spirits and Earth Mother. Expanded awareness became a natural part of her life on earth. She recognized that life on earth and in the Great Beyond creates a continuum of frequency. Also, she realized that crossing the threshold requires similar conscious awareness. Patricia welcomes this multidimensional aspect of her soul as a precious part of wholeness, which is our birthright.

Patricia holds an M.A. from Texas Woman's University and a B.A from the University of Maryland. She is a trained BioAcoustics Research Associate (BARA) in sound healing. Patricia lives in the high mountains west of Boulder, Colorado with her daughter and pets.

You can reach the author, Patricia L'Dara, at:
www.soulpassagemidwife.com.

www.ingramcontent.com/pod-product-compliance
Lightning Source LLC
Chambersburg PA
CBHW062155080426
42734CB00010B/1703